ASHTAR

REVEALING THE SECRET IDENTITY OF THE FORCES OF LIGHT & THEIR SPIRITUAL PROGRAM FOR EARTH

Compiled by Tuella
Inner Light Publications

ISBN: 0-938294-29-6

Editorial Direction
& Layout
Timothy Green Beckley

Cover Art by Celaya Winkler

Composition and design:
Cross-Country Consultants
8858 E. Palm Ridge Drive
Scottsdale, AZ 85260

For permission to reprint specific portions or to inquire
about foreign rights, address request to Inner Light, Box 753,
New Brunswick, NJ 08903

Free catalog of books upon request.

Dedication

This book is lovingly dedicated to Ashtar,
a friend and brother and my beloved Commander,
with whom I serve the kingdom of God on earth
and the Light of Our Radiant One.

Tuella

Preface

It has been both my great honor and my joyful assigned task to assemble within the covers of this book, many of the most vital communications received by spiritual messengers from Commander Ashtar since his earliest contacts with our dimension.

To have included them all would have been an impossible task. Rather we have attempted to compile those fragments which would best help us to discern the heart of this beloved Being, to appreciate his spiritual burden, his exemplary character, his depth of purpose, his unswerving loyalty to Our Radiant One and his dedication to the Kingdom of God on Earth.

May the aura of his Light and his Love touch you as you read, to enjoy, to absorb, to be quickened to new heights of spiritual understanding and attainment.

—Tuella

Foreword

We are the voices of those who serve with Commander Ashtar of the Ashtar Command. We send forth this combined tribute to our beloved Leader. We commend the efforts of this Messenger to compile and give to the world this tribute and file of information which will greatly enlighten many to the mass efforts of all our fleets for the benefit of planet Earth, regardless of our origin from outer Space.

Our love for the people of Earth and the planet has motivated our participation with Beloved Commander Jesus Sananda and Commander Ashtar, in this tremendous Program for the benefit of humankind. Our volunteer efforts stem from a dedication to brighten the Lighted Pathway for all souls everywhere, and to be contributing units of the Brotherhood of Light in this sector of Space.

We have jointly followed the leadings of our Commanders down through the ages, through two to three generations within our own families who have also served the Hierarchy in this Mission. Our families, our children and spiritual mates, have in most cases remained behind on our home systems until this Earth mission is fulfilled and its splendor and beauty unfolds within its new dimension of glory.

The battle is not yet completed, the victory is not yet attained, but we know that the influence of Ashtar throughout our ranks, will guide the Hierarchal Program through the coming tumultuous restoration with wisdom and foresight, courage and ultimate victory. The people of Earth will receive the highest spiritual enlightenment, the planet will be cleansed, the clutches of those who seek to destroy will be lost and removed and the Kingdom of God shall come to Earth as it is in Heaven.

Under the coordinating leadership of the Ashtar Command, our scattered energies and various factions have been fused to one united channel of divine force, with strong guidance in the many indescribable details and challenges of the Great Mission. All of the various fields of patrol, whether it be scientific, educational, spiritual or protective, have been coordinated into one vast unified expression of cooperation and accomplishment. The last two decades have brought the placement of many new bases set into operation. The multitude of fleets small and great, have served as one, in the pattern of the leadership expanded before us.

In the face of any great divine challenge, the Radiant One chooses one great Man. In our fields of endeavor, Ashtar has been that Man. His energies have increased the efficiency of all of our individual responsibilities to a point beyond description. We have honored this Man in our midst and followed his guidance with respect. His love for mankind has consistently been his motivation.

His spiritual emanations and philosophical teachings have been an inspiration to all of us as well as to all of you. His intense devotional nature has been an example throughout all of the fleets. His wisdom in lifting the vibrations of the planet while yielding to none in his adamant plea for the respect of the right of man to choose his way without outside interference in his growth.

We can do naught but follow Ashtar to the ultimate Conclusion of the Battle for the Light. We are the Etherians of this Universe and its many Galaxies, who have come together in this volunteer effort for planet Earth. Many of us are with you now in physical form for this crucial time in your transformation. Many are yet to come to fill in the ranks, but all stand with appreciation, beside the Leader Our Radiant One has chosen, to lead this offensive for the Forces of Light in the Program of man's ascension.

It is with a sincere desire for his honor, that we jointly form this statement to express our love for Commander Ashtar, and we speak for the many. We call for the blessings of the Higher Guardians to bless this Tribute as it is placed in the hands of the people of Earth. May the love of Ashtar, as it is shown to be given freely to all men, return to his own bosom a thousandfold in blessings of Peace. Peace on Earth and Goodwill to all men will surely come with Ashtar at the helm of the Mission.

Speaking for the entire constituency of the Ashtar Command, its many great fleets and officers, and the thousands who make up the ranks and the souls who inhabit the millions of worlds of this Universe, we are

Soltec of the Scientific Patrols
Monka of the Tribunal Councils
Korton of the Communications Service Athena
of the Starship of Sananda

1
Ashtar...The Man

Who Is Ashtar

Man or Myth? Name or Title? Space Commander or Archanger? Intergalactic Spiritual Leader? We believe that the pursuit of these answers will be an interesting adventure to those dedicated to understanding the Guardian Action surrounding this planet,

In the voluminous transmissions received by Dr. Enid Smith, UFO pioneer extraordinaire, Ashtar was often referred to as the *Christian Commander from Venus*. In our initial issue of UNIVERSAL NETWORK, in an item dictated by Lord Michael (through Gabriel Green), Michael refers to Ashtar' as the *"Supreme Director in charge of all of the Spiritual Program"* for our planet.

Under the sponsorship of Lord Michael and the Great Central Sun government of this galaxy, Commander Ashtar is second only to the Beloved Commander Jesus-Sananda in responsibility for the airborne division of the Brotherhood of Light. Ashtar has been widely known in UFO channeling circles for over three decades. His messages are beamed from a colossal Starship, or Space Station, beyond our atmosphere. He is loved for his deeply philosophical approach to our global problems and his efforts to raise our planetary vibrations.

Ashtar speaks of twenty million extraterrestrial persons involved with his Command in the Program for planet Earth, and of another four million on our physical plane, consciously or unconsciously cooperating in the program of Light.

I was curious about his alleged Venusian beginnings, and

he volunteered: "I am of that strain of Beings who have manifested from that chain of planets, the lesser of which is known to you as *Venus*. However, the planet *Ashtar* was my original manifestation through the Father's love."

I pressed for further personal information, and was not disappointed. "The mystery that is associated with my person is of no consequence to me, but is perhaps of interest to some. I am seven feet tall in height, with blue eyes and a nearly white complexion. I am fast of movement and considered to be an understanding and compassionate leader. I am devoted to the principles and teachings of Our Radiant One, and I represent the Twelfth Kingdom and the Great Central Sun Hierarchy. I have been assigned the name of 'Ashtar' by that Universal Hierarchy for use in my calling as Commander of the Intergalactic fleets serving this hemisphere.

"I have not had a human embodiment upon planet Earth, as some have inferred. This is incorrect information and should be discouraged. I have consistently been too involved with the affairs of the Universe to accept such an assignment. I am an active member of Councils scattered throughout this Universal Sector, serving in an advisory capacity at strategic levels of intergalactic affairs.

"The fleets of Etheria stationed within the Sector known as *Schare*, represent what is now called the Confederation of Planets for Peace. We are a branch of the greater Federation of Free Worlds which comprises the totality of the Space Commands throughout the Omniverse. While my own administration is local to the Commands of this solar system, I am not restricted to this sector in my service, for I represent our system in the councils of other galaxies and universes throughout the vast cosmos. From time to time I have been appointed to positions of higher responsibilities in those councils.

"The Christ Teacher of this galaxy is my Beloved Commander in Chief, and His Word is my Law. To Him I have pledged my service. I am but a leader chosen by Him, to fulfill

11

the Program of Light on Earth through the winged commands of the Great Brotherhood. Each one of us is an active member of the pact taken by personal vow to serve that Cause."

Reflecting upon the general outline of this book, I confessed to mixed emotions concerning the advisability of reprinting messages with which so many would already be familiar—at least, the senior members of this movement. Ashtar replied: "I feel very impersonal toward the material. I am only concerned that it be read by a broad segment of ready souls and that it be given serious consideration. A thing worth saying is worth having repeated. Anything that is worth repeating is worth fixing attention upon. The messages of the past, as well as the present, carry the same burden of concern for humankind. We do not change our concern with the passing of time. A call of twenty or even thirty years ago is just as valid this day. Our messages have found a more tolerant audience at this time. Because of the ongoing exchange. Nevertheless, the need for them is crucial at this hour—not only for a further emphasis, but for the benefit of those who may not have seen them at all.

"Therefore, in their repetition, further enlightenment will come to those who search at this hour. Be vigilant, my friend, in season and out of season, to spread the good will of your Brothers and Friends from Outer Dimensions of the Cosmos. We are all the Children of God, together under one banner and One Mission of Light. We join forces to bring this newest effort into manifestation. Regardless of the source, the words are Light, and they are Truth. We release them again for the Glory of God! The compiled content will reveal the nature of the messages through the decades as having had a *certain theme,* regardless of the channel, and it will contribute to an understanding of our reality and purpose in being with men, to plead with them to experience love and good will toward one another. There are presently many new students awakening with a lack of familiarity of the earliest contacts. Further, the book will contain extraterrestrial information in general, needed by these new candidates in the mission."

• • •

With this extra bit of polishing touch upon my vision, I was fired with inspired enthusiasm to get started on the project. In summary, we repeat this paragraph from the early pages of *Project: World Evacuation*:

"Ashtar is a Beloved Christian Commander and a very beautiful Being. He is highly evolved in the upper worlds, very influential, and has a great beneficial influence upon those he leads. The momentum of the vibrations from these Great Space Beings, or Commanders, as they call themselves, is equal to and often beyond the force-field even of Ascended Masters, for many have come who are Lords on their own planet, or persons of highest repute in their own galaxies and dimensions."

• • •

Considering Ashtar's Appearance

On the following page is a pen line sketch of Ashtar done by artist Carol Rodriguez. The light long hair and the characteristic high forehead were of interest to me. The sternness of his manner is given attention in the treatment of the cheeks and bone structure. This artist once made the statement in describing these Great Ones: "Their radiant auras obscure details, thus causing them to often be seen differently by different people." This is very true, and we trust you will bear with us as we attempt to correlate several familiar interpretations of Ashtar.

We were indeed grateful to artist Celaya Winkler for her permission to feature her painting of Ashtar upon our cover. And our thanks also to Ida Partridge, owner of the painting—a part of her private collection—for her graciousness and willingness to share it.

Celaya personally feels very close to Ashtar and his love and wisdom, and his desire to help planet Earth in its transition. She has the intuitive ability to receive impressions that are her guidance in portrait work. The cover portrait interestingly includes his helmet, which is a necessary part of their intergalactic communication system. In my own private collection, a painting of Athena contains the same pointed feature atop her helmet also. Almost all interpretations do include the crew collar effect at the neck of his uniform. I dared to ask him if, in his opinion, the cover painting was a reasonable rendition of

ASHTAR

From the book *New World Order,* published by Global Communications, New York. Art by Carol Rodriguez.

his appearance. "Fairly so. The uniform and helmet are absolutely accurate. The lighted circles represent a personal vortex in connection with the Radiant One. The complexion is very fair in your terms—more so than the rendition suggests— which is considerably darker at the shadows and the eyes. Eyebrows could be just a bit lighter and more fair, and the eyes a lighter blue, which is characteristic of residents of this chain of planets referred to earlier."

A friend in France was kind enough to share these following sketches of "Ashtar Sheran" as drawn by the young German medium of the Speer family in Berlin in 1957 and used in the book *De Jules Verne Aux Extra Terrestres,* by M. Chotard. (Refer to the two following pages). Here the now-famous widow's peak, so often mentioned by clairvoyants, is clearly seen. The front view has the hair in almost identical appearance as I described in the opening chapter of the Evacuation manuscript.

In 1973 Eugenio Siragusa, an Italian contactee, shared his spiritual image of Ashtar with an artist (unknown) to give us the next interpretation. In better reproductions the hair appears to be short and close to the scalp. Be that as it may, nevertheless, the confirming facial characteristics are unmistakable. We like a change of hair style occasionally; shall we deny our space friends the same privilege?

Our final rendition, in a somewhat abstract vein, was done by a French artist (possibly also a medium), Danielle Lecluc, just a few years ago. In spite of its style, certain features still consistently dominate.

All of these interesting contributions combine to give us a fairly accurate idea of the features of Commander Ashtar.

ASHTAR SHERAN
Reproduction exécutée par le médium

ASHTAR SHERAN
Reproduction exécutée par le médium

ASHTAR
As seenby Eugenio Siragusa

ASHTAR

As painted by Danielle Le Cluc

The Etherians

In 1958 Trevor James released *They Live in the Sky,* published by Dr. Franklin Thomas through New Age Publishing Company. The book contained several fascinating and informative interviews with Ashtar. Mr. James poses direct questions to the Commander:

Question: "Are you etheric beings? Or are you possessed of a fleshly physical body such as mine?"

Ashtar: "I am etheric. I do not have a fleshly body like yours, bounded by flesh. But it is possible for me to make my being visible to your optics by certain changes in its vibratory rate."

Question: "This would mean, then, that you are normally invisible to us?"

Ashtar: "Yes."

If we take Ashtar at his word, we have explanations for some of the alleged encounters with space beings, and also for the fact that both ships and controlling intelligences are known to be invisible on occasions. These beings can convert to a vibratory rate where they are visible to us, but normally belong in a higher vibration.

Question: "As you are an etheric being, are other etheric beings visible to you?"

Ashtar: "Yes, although not exactly in terms of optical vision as you know it."

It was about eighteen months after this communication had been received that I gained a rather startling proof of its validity. I paid a call on a distinguished European lady in Los Angeles with an international reputation as a seer and psychic. Discussing various aspects of her faculty with me and answering my questions, she suddenly sat bolt upright in her chair. "Have you ever had any contact with any non-physical beings?" she asked, with a smile. I replied that I believed that I had, but could not be completely sure.

She then said, "There is a magnificent looking being standing beside you, and he communicates to me that is name is Ashtar. Do you know him?"

I replied that the personality was familiar, and she gave me a full *description of him as she saw him clairvoyantly*. Seven feet or so tall, extremely stern, helmeted, and giving the impression of being a sort of military man.

This was extremely interesting insofar as Ashtar had described himself as the "Commandant, Vela Quadra Sector, Realms of Schare, All Projections, All Waves," and therefore would probably be a military type of being.

In possession of just the beginnings of these general theories, I addressed further questions to Ashtar on this subject.

Question: "From your statement that you are etheric, am I to presume that you have evolved beyond the stage of a physical and astral body?"

Ashtar: "Correct. I do not possess a physical casing of the dense type such as yours. I am definitely etheric, *as are all people on other planets in this solar system*. However, this does not mean that we are invisible to each other as we are to you under normal circumstances. We see each other and live much as you do, but we do not have this dense physical casing which you possess. The advantages, benefits and comforts of this living are enormous, and the irritations of the fleshly envelope are most uncomfortable. Unless we *choose* to convert the vibrational frequency of our bodies to one which is visible to your optics, we remain invisible to your people. Highly evolved people, with a good 'psychic eye' as you call it, can sometimes see us in vaporous form, although we may be invisible to other earthlings in the same location. When your clairvoyants travel to our civilizations on other planets, they see and are able to interpret our lives because they are not using their physical eyes but their astral or psychic sight, to which we are visible just as though we were physical."

Question: "When you become visible to our eyes does the person who sees you know that you are a 'converted etheric'?"

Ashtar: "Not as a rule. The conversion can be made so completely that a physical person encountering us thinks that we, too, are physical."

Question: "What of those who claim to have been up in your craft?"

Ashtar: "In our contacts with earthlings we have to be careful not to go beyond their understanding. In these instances, the ships and all entities within them are converted to a vibrational level at which they have the substance of physical things as known to you. Whether the experience was physical or astral is not known to some people who had the experience."

Question: "I wish to ask a question or two concerning etheric substance."

Ashtar: "We will be glad to answer whatever we can for you. We wish to arm you with as much knowledge as possible, and are limited in this only by your power to assimilate it. I do not wish to talk over your head, but we will supply you with knowledge to the limit of your understanding."

Question: "I am puzzled by the concept of etheric matter. For example, there is one case on record where one of our jet aircraft flew right through a space ship without hitting anything solid whatever. Are your ships made of a vaporous substance, or are they a different form of earthly matter?"

Ashtar: "We have all the elements you know on earth, and many more. The etheric form of these metals differs in its atomic and molecular structure from earth-made metals. For example, the distance between the nucleus and the orbiting electrons of the etheric iron nucleus is much greater than in iron as you know it on earth. This permits the atoms of earthly steel to pass right through the atoms of etheric steel in such a way nothing happens to either form of steel. The etheric form of steel enjoys a higher vibratory rate than earthly steel and therefore is not apparent to earthly vision or, if you prefer, physical eyesight. Under certain circumstances it becomes visible, as in the presence of certain atmospheric gases of Shan (Earth) or at will in accordance with the desire of the controlling intelligence. No matter how great the mass of the etheric substance, even a space ship measuring many miles across in your measure, physical matter cannot damage or injure it or its contents."

Question: "When you speak of making etheric matter visible at will, is this the way that George Adamski was permitted to take his now-famous photographs?"

Ashtar: "Yes. Ether ships, as they have been called on your surface, have been made visible to and for certain individuals, selected upon your surface, of whom Adamski is one. *Normally,* the ships are part of the *invisible* world."

Question: "If one were to develop astral vision or the psychic eye, would he be able to see the ships?"

Ashtar: "No. Not unless the vibratory rate of the ship were converted to the vibratory range of astral vision. Remember, the etheric vibratory rate is higher than the astral. Very few physical humans have some perception of the etheric, but they are not normal people as you know them and for the most part dwell in very secluded places. As a general rule, perception of the etheric through vision cannot be accomplished except through the will of the etheric, converting etheric substance to a vibratory level where it is physically visible."

Question: "In our solar system, are there any other physical beings like us?"

Ashtar: "No. All beings on other planets in your solar system are etherics. On your planet, as you now know, there are

24

two kinds of beings, physical and astral. Outside the earth-moon system in your solar system, all are etheric."

• • •

(Although the following interview does not involve Ashtar personally, its information is so pertinent, it is included.)

Question: "I would like you to give your description of the differences between space people and spirit people. I would appreciate as full an answer as my understanding permits."

Andolo: "The differences are very great, although to the cursory glance it may seem that space people are spirits. However, it all comes down to a matter of the condition in which we dwell. We are etheric beings, in your expression. By this, I mean that we live upon a higher plane of existence. We are not discarnate in the sense of having *no* bodies. We have etheric bodies which are counterparts of your bodies but which are made of a more tenuous substance, and which are not subject in the same way to gravitational effects. The etheric state in which we dwell is one of many on an ascending evolutionary scale to which we all belong.

"Above us, for example, are beings more highly evolved than us by as great a gap as there is between ourselves and you. This is not meant in any derogatory sense towards you, but merely as a factual statement about the scales on which we dwell. Upon our plane of life we have much the same type of existence as you do, although it is free of the corruptions, crimes and undesirable elements which are to be worked out of a being's karmic life before he may pass into the etheric state. Your earth is a testing ground—one of many hundreds of thousands of testing grounds in the Universe—where beings evolve upwards on the scale of life, working constantly towards junction with the Great One as the ultimate attainment of all existence. We upon the etheric planes pass on to higher planes just as you do from earth, when qualified. This transformation on your plane is termed 'death.'

"To us, it is merely a transformer interposed between us and the next level of life to which we will ascend. We will stress once more that the greatest factor in the way of a proper grasp of the true story of life on your planet is the conception of death as the end of all existence. Nothing could be further from the truth. Upon your plane, you must serve out an evolutionary period before you can ascend to higher worlds. The fleshly bodies which you have are part of a plan to aid your working through this scale of existence. At your level you must endure savage crimes, wars, strife and violence, and the Great One, in His wisdom, has seen fit to use the fleshly body as the most convenient method of taking care of this almost elemental stage of existence. Now then, there are more people waiting to serve out their karmic penalties than there are physical casings, or bodies, to go around. Therefore, there is a dwelling place around your planet for these bodiless entities from your surface. These are spirits, or spirit people. They are, if you like, in suspension, or their evolution is interrupted, and they are anxious to return to the body either to carry out something they left undone, or else, after realizing the truth or partial truth of creation, to become incarnate again and work towards proper passage through earthly life prior to ascending to higher realms.

"We are in bodies of a tenuous but nonetheless real substance, vibrating at a rate much greater than that which prevails on your planet. Spirit people are dwellers in astral form who cannot go beyond that astral form without serving out their karmic life in a casing of flesh as you know it. Communication is possible, both with us and the spirit people. But in communicating with spirits you may find that they know but little more than earth dwellers, and in many cases, not as much. They may have nothing valid to impart. They may play tricks and jokes upon people contacting them. Therefore we can only suggest that all such communications be done with extreme care and *with a reason*. Without reason behind it, it is little more than folly. I leave you in love and good will. I am Andolo."

26

Ashtar's Personal Frequency

It is one thing to understand the etheric nature of a Being; it is another matter to know his personal vibrational keynote. What is Ashtar really like beneath his seeming militant demeanor?

As a Universal Statesman of wide renown, his policies of nonintervention and support of man's right of choice are respected and supported. He deplores the manipulation tactics of the world illuminati and its grip upon mankind.

Hermes, the Great Master of Wisdom, has a loving comment to share with us:

"I speak in my capacity as Universal Teacher of many things. I join with you in honoring one who has been in service with us for a longer time than I can remember. Our Beloved Brother in the Light, Ashtar, has been one for whom I have had much respect and admiration. We have learned in the spiritual Hierarchy that we can depend upon him to discharge a task with dependability, responsibility and ingenious expertise.

"In his earliest venturing forth from Venus on this appointed task to serve the Universe by lifting the vibrations of this planet, he was a most courteous and benevolent volunteer. I recall his genuine eagerness to place himself at the disposal of Michael and the Central Sun Hierarchy. He was immediately accepted, for his record on his home planets of Venus and Ashtar (a planet) were exemplary and noteworthy. He stationed himself immediately at the right hand of the Beloved, and has, one might almost say, never left that position—at

27

least, theoretically. He is a staunch defender of the Truth as taught by the Master and an ardent foe of its opposition. He has been well trained by Michael in the subtleties of dealing with the brothers of the lefthanded path. He respects them as part of the Father's Creation, but fearlessly deals with their devastating programs and will not tolerate their restrictions of man's freedom."

• • •

Commander Ashtar has labored tirelessly to give humanity guidelines for a better way of life. He acclaims the freedom of man to choose his pathway without interference. He has repeatedly held council with the Ascended Masters Godfrey and St. Germain in the interest of freedom for America, and valiantly stood in the pathway of forces designed to restrict that freedom. But the concern for individual freedom goes deeper than any national principle. It reflects the unimpeachable and inherent right of every soul, the freedom of will to choose its pathway, its mistakes, and its karma.

Later in the text we will cite the messages through Mrs. Hill, but for now, let me quote an interesting passage which reveals further some of Ashtar's inner convictions:

"My message concerns a number of erroneous claims being made by those who crave personal publicity. Anyone who may attempt to invest us with powers of divination and announce themselves the recipients of information pertaining to the *private* affairs of individuals *(unless* they apply specifically to serious national or international matters) is guilty of falsification. Only insofar as they affect our plans (which must of necessity depend to a considerable extent on the understanding and cooperation of dwellers on your planet) will we pay any attention to your own purely personal problems by prying into the future for answers to your queries."

This was borne out in a statement given to me recently:

"Souls must struggle with their own growth problems as

every other soul has ever had to do. We have not indulged in *fortune telling as a sponsored activity because of the need of the soul to make its own choices and decisions if it is to over- come the labyrinth of life's temptations. Thus, guidance is not intended to interfere nor hinder the freedom of man's will to choose his pathway.* Only in this manner does he ascend the lower nature and the lesser level of living. We strongly adhere to the freedom of man to be exercised and permitted without interference from another."

• • •

Commander Soltec offers further insight concerning Ashtar:

"In the beginning of our organization of the earliest fleets, we did not have a large quantity of craft for earth supervision. We approached Commander Ashtar and asked him how we could possibly efficiently patrol such a large area with such a small task force. His reply was succinct: 'We will endeavor to expand ourselves and to be everywhere at once with our unlim- ited abilities to do so.' This is an example of the dogged deter- mination of the Man to do his very best in any situation. And we did just that! We did not rely upon our craft, but we entered into the highest possible use of the gifts that were within us, and we expanded our highest level of being to literally be where we were not, and to see what we could not and to hear what we could not hear, and altogether became the eyes of God surrounding the planet. Eventually more craft were added, divisions of responsibilities were assigned, and the mission expanded continually unto the point of tremendous scope that it is today. But I have never forgotten my Commander's words who, nothing daunted, would make a way where there was no way.

"It has been a tremendous experience to me, serving with him and carefully following his example in many details of our shared responsibilities. I have often paused in troubling instances to ask myself, 'How would Ashtar handle this problem?' Invariably the answer would be clarified and I have found it has always proven the wisest course of action to have taken. The mention of Ashtar's name has sometimes brought a shadow of staunch militarism into a conversation in the past, because the nature of his dedication to the Armies of Light is so intense it is reflected in his manner with people. This has sometimes erroneously been interpreted as a sternness of demeanor, a strict formality, so to speak; but in actuality, this is not the case. I have never known a more loving, gentle man when it comes to the application of divine love toward his fellow man. His eye is so single to victory for the forces of Light, he is sometimes misunderstood. Those who first have contact with him sense this firmness of purpose, but soon come to know and love the deeper aspects of his gentleness. We have all found it to be so.

"My surveillance responsibilities have been unlike Ashtar's in that my mission is the gathering of facts and scientific data that can in turn be used for the betterment of humanity and this solar system. The mission of Ashtar has been the spiritual education of a backward planet and the ascension of its inhabitants through initiations and gathering of information designed for that purpose. Nevertheless, we have enjoyed a very close friendship and respect for one another's work in the overall divine program. It is an honor to be a part of the mission of the Ashtar Command. I am Soltec."

• • •

A disciple speaks:

"Greetings, my beloved daughter. These wonderful thoughts are being shared with you at last and I am pleased. Now I have come in tonight to offer my statement for the book. In the Christian era, Ashtar was placed in command of the great star ship which brought and released the soul of Jesus and again, received Him up when His mission was completed.

He has ever been that one in command of the starship which is peculiarly the etheric navigational vehicle for the Beloved Master. That is the fact I wanted to stress for this evening. I am Philip, of the Christian era of history."

Spaceman or Angel?

Many are intrigued by the mystique of the true Celestial identity not only of Ashtar, but also of the many great Space intelligences we have come to know and love by the names assigned to them in the Divine Program.

I, too, attempted to probe this mystery of Ashtar's Universal status, but the persistent reluctance to discuss personal matters is constant:

"The Mission to be accomplished is the factor of import and not the spiritual status of the one who serves that Mission. Like all of my other Brothers and Sisters in the Program of Light, we are not to be worshiped or thought of as Gods or anything of that nature. We are simply your comrades in the Light of the Radiant One, equal all, in the sight of the Creator. It is regrettable that there is a tendency of humanity to focus attention upon a messenger rather than upon the message. Overemphasis on personal revelation weakens the strength of the Mission, which is geared to the spiritual growth of mankind."

Contactee Oscar Magocsi, of Canada, has submitted an interesting brief commentary, received through his Psychean Federation sources, when Ashtar's changed identity as Gabriel was under discussion:

"Commander Ashtar has many roles. He is Protector and Defender, Advisor and Administrator, but his work as Protector and Defender is the most prominent. A Commander is one who speaks with Authority to command and issue orders. Ashtar is a Protector of humanity and the fate of planet Earth, as well as a

Defender-Protector of the Solar System and its affairs.

"However, in the strictest sense, he is not an *embodiment* of an Archangel, but is, nevertheless, participating in a very close partnership and very close cooperative cosmic representation of one of high administration at that level. It is not Archangel Gabriel, but is another. Within his own attributes of Protector, Defender and Enforcer, another Archangel works in unison with the energies of Ashtar."

With characteristic ambiguity, this Federation source refused to reveal the actual identity of Ashtar's overshadowing Presence, but did clearly state that the Commander was being guided by an Archangel OTHER than Gabriel, in a very personal way, and that the prominence of the Defender and Protector roles should be a clue to the wise, in the full revelation. In spite of an inner nagging that this raised more questions than it answered, I felt comfortable with the information and wanted to share it with you.

Gray Barker has an important observation in his introduction to the E.P. Hill book, published by the Saucerian Press:

"Modern metaphysics, although it has helped thousands, made them more self-reliant, positive in their thinking, intellectually mature and responsible, nevertheless, has practically ignored the fact that there are beings in this Universe besides ourselves—beings which the ancients sometimes called 'Angels,' and who are now being called 'Space Men.' All down the ages there have been mystics who claimed to have heard the VOICE OF GOD or of Angels. Today there are those who hear the voice of Space Men."

The fascinating concept that links the Extraterrestrial Armies with the work of the angels, whom the Heavenly Father charged to watch over those who would be the HEIRS OF SALVATION, is inspiring to consider.

At a group meeting in Prescott, Arizona, questions were put to trance medium Bob Graham, by someone as a test, who wanted to hear from another source just who Ashtar was.

33

Joshua was the source of the transmission, received clairaudiently by Bob. The session went like this:

Question: "Who is Ashtar?"

Answer: "Ashtar is of the herald angels and first manifested in the early '50s through so-called UFO type of communications with individuals like George van Tassel and others, awaiting the return of the herald angels, who are the participants in the so-called UFOs that have 'manifested' from time to time. They are observing from their sphere which is not physical the actions of men and nations as the periods of time ripen for the return of the Christ, who will return on those same clouds of heaven, which are partial or full materializations of the vehicles used in the celestial realms.

"Ashtar is known to have materialized, and also, his craft has materialized. They refer to our planet as planet Sector Schare. The ancients of old would have referred to them as the 'herald angels.' Ashtar and others, including Excelsior, are a very vital link between the various celestial spheres and our own in this great network of holy spirits, whose primary function is to enlighten mankind.

"They also play a very important role in preserving the United States from extinction by warring forces that are soon to attack its shores. That only by this divine intervention will the enemy be driven, and that the destiny of the United States will be assured as the example that will be set as Christ returns, and that this nation will serve mankind until the end time when the physical universe is no longer needed and is dissolved back into its ethereal form.

"Ashtar also represents one of countless hosts similar to those who manifested in the times of Isaiah and slew thousands of Philistines in the preservation of the Israelites. The history of the dawn of man records countless manifestations of these herald angels."

Question: "Did Ashtar ever live on Earth?"

Answer: "He is not part of the fallen spirits, and though

34

there are individuals not understanding the nature of the gifts that they received and of the nature of the difference between the physical and spiritual realms, subscribe that he is of a much higher planet than this, and others subscribe that Ashtar and others like him are those who evolved from this planet, this is not the case with Ashtar or other herald angels, who did not take part in the great spiritual revolt, but remained loyal to God and to Christ. They are the holy spirits who are assigned to this sphere from time to time in guiding mankind back to God. Having never tasted spiritual death, they have always been among the living who dwelled with God.

"And, I might add, that before this generation is through, you will observe the greatest celestial activity ever witnessed on this planet, as these so-called 'clouds of heaven,' which are merely a condensation of those vehicles, arrive in great numbers and defy your wind as they remain, or oppose it. That is why it is mentioned that Christ's return shall be on the clouds of heaven. They are the vehicles, when fully materialized; are great, gleaming, metallic, crystalline vehicles used in the great, enormous outreaches of the celestial realms."

The above transmission (which was shared with me by a friend) is of tremendous significance when coupled with a message from Lord Jesus-Sananda which was used as the FORE-WORD in the *Project: World Evacuation* volume. In referring specifically to our Beloved Space Friends, the Master said:

"These come as My Angels, to reap that which has been sown, to divide and set asunder the tares from the wheat, to gather the wheat into My Barn. For I AM the householder who cometh at the end of the day for an account from His Servants, and to give to all men justly in the manner given by them to Me.

"Those who come IN MY Name go from heart to heart, sealing them against that day and marking them for deliverance and safety from all that would destroy.

"So, I shall call unto those who follow Me, to listen to the voices of these who come from other worlds, and harden not your hearts against their words or practices. Rather, lift up LOVE unto them and desire for their coming, for THEY ARE THE ANGELS OF THE HARVEST!

"I AM SANANDA, AND THIS IS MY MESSAGE TO THE WORLD."

• • •

Long after I had come to personally know Commander Ashtar and to love and respect him, it was no small shock to me when for the first time, someone reproached me with, "There's no such person, that's just a title."' My assailant actually, sincerely believed this close-minded statement, having read it somewhere in the past, and not having known the Commander personally. This soul has long since now come to know Ashtar as I know him, but at the time, it was disturbing to discover such a heresy actually existed.

At the earliest opportunity for an appointment, I confronted Ashtar with these things. He quietly and calmly replied:

"I am Ashtar; it is my name and not an office; I am a person, even as you are a person, and not a title; I exist and am not a myth; I am not a nonentity, neither am I from the second density; I am a being and not an influence; a soldier of the Light and not a ghost. Yes I have had many imitators, but stronghearted ones have not been deceived for that is impossible. Accusers have sought to bring reproach upon my name as a designed strategy, but I continue on faithfully, doing my duty to God and His Creation.

"When we are busy in dedicated service to the cause of Light, we have neither the time nor the energy to pause to waste on our ever-present critics and attackers. The mud of unjust judgments falls away as you run the race. It does not and has not perturbed my demeanor when accusations have been formed to discredit my words or my person."

It was difficult for me to understand how such a concept

could be held for a long period of time, even by the most sincere, without having a proper explanation given to that one. Ashtar graciously explained:

"Discrepancy naturally enters when souls are quick to accept what another has said, to enlarge and dogmatize the thought form. If the mired then closes upon this finalized version of a concept (without further personal research or *openness to discussion*) then any further explanation, clarification or understanding is rendered unsuccessful. When a *false crystallization* has therefore taken place, those who would otherwise attempt a clarification simply withdraw until further growth takes place. Remember the Beloved. Though his own clearly understood His person, yet...ere the cock crowed thrice...did deny Him."

The following day, however, when Commander Korton tuned into my thoughts, his thoughts were not so calm:

"As ridiculous as it may sound that some would say Ashtar didn't exist, you can readily understand the mountain of opposition this would cancel if it could be made believable. The genesis is that those who *do not know him* can be bent by every wind. Those who know him cannot be moved."

(Immediately my mind recounted the question of the Master to His disciple: "Whom do men say that I am?" There was apparently varied opinion, but those who knew had a heavenly revelation of His identity). Korton continued:

"I highly respect this great Universal Leader and appreciate all that he has done, as one individual, toward the liberation of mankind from all that would bind him to lesser levels of attainment. Under the benediction of Lord Michael, of the Great Central Sun Government, Ashtar has guided the Divine Program of Enlightenment for this world, devotedly serving in his task beside Our Beloved Commander, Jesus-Sananda.

"It would be impossible for one so consumed with dedication to a cause, and out front in its offensive, to not draw to himself the fire of those whose strategy would be to discredit his person and thereby destroy his influence.

"In your land, those voices that are raised in the interest of freedom for all men, who have any influencing force of note, are soon slain or removed. Great ones of your dimension who have attempted to raise their voices in the cause of freedom eventually fall into the hands of their assassins.

"Let me picture an analogy. When your world faced a common threat, a common enemy of freedom, and the challenge had to be met and conquered, forces gathered from Australia, from France. They poured in from America, from England. These various forces did not reason, 'I think I'll fight the enemy at such and such a place at such and such a time,' or perhaps another force decide, 'I will engage the enemy and dispose of the threat on this front of force when I get time,' or America likewise did not *alone* decide to combat the enemy at a certain Location. No. Rather, they all joined forces, united their various commands and worked together in their challenge as the Allied Command!

"Order, not disorder; organization, not chaos. Various great Commanding Leaders joined their wits and means, men and equipment in united offense as one Command—THE ALLIED COMMAND. Do you think that we of the higher worlds are any less capable than ye of Earth? Would we not also disdain disorder and chaos, we who can see beyond what you can see, know beyond what you know? Would we not also see the value of joining our scattered energies into one united effort toward the goal of guarding and guiding Earth? Therefore, as your Allied Command had its Eisenhower, *so our Allied Command has its Ashtar!* All Commanders work in unison and love throughout the Galaxy. Thus do we strive as one, as do you who serve this Light from your dimension. We are all one in purpose and unity for the incoming Kingdom of God on Earth. I apologize for my vociferous response, or abundance of words, which cometh only from the abundance of the heart. I am Commander Korton, proudly serving the forces of Ashtar in the light of our Radiant One. Adonai."

It seemed this discussion could not be put to rest without one further comment, which soon followed from Lord Michael:

"This book is important to us because of the diabolical influence of the dark ones in their attacks upon my own Lieutenant Commander, Ashtar. This, his name, has been given to him in his service to the Celestial Government for the closing of this age. As one of my chief ranking assistants in celestial realms, he has a higher name.

"I, Michael, do, without reservation, wholeheartedly endorse the work of Ashtar in the Name of the Brotherhood of Light. As Universal Statesman and Ambassador, his efforts have the fullest extent of my Authority behind them. Our governing Spiritual Hierarchy has commissioned him to his task and sent him forth as an able representative of the policies and program set in order by that Hierarchy. I stand behind his efforts, his decisions and his works, to defend and protect, to educate and exhort the race of mankind to lift themselves higher in their aspirations and desires to walk the Christ Pathway as torches of Light.

"We of the Governing Body of this Universe have found it necessary and proficient to enlist the services of these many highly endowed individuals who have chosen this service as a gesture of brotherhood, to assist your planet and thereby guide the destiny of the entire Solar System into a higher dimension of life.

"The day will come when the men of Earth will rise up and call him blessed who has served as leader of this volunteer force, guided their coordination, broadcast their messages to Earth in a multitude of ways, to spread the good news of the Kingdom of God on Earth. We salute the Ashtar Command and all that it embodies, as well as all that it has accomplished and shall accomplish for the fulfillment of the Will of God. Receive ye this great man, with our blessings and our benediction. I an Michael, of the Lord's Hosts."

Breaking The Sound Barrier

On July 18, 1952, George van Tassel made UFO history. Following much self discipline and continual contact from various other Space intelligences, and coinciding with plans in the scientific community to explode the hydrogen element, on that date, Mr. van Tassel was warned by a being called "Portla" that their Chief was about to enter this solar system FOR THE FIRST TIME.

Then followed the first message from Commander Ashtar to this planet. In his initial contact, Ashtar gave his specific identity, his rank, and his base of operations. This historical statement is printed in full in Winfield Brownell's book, *UFOs, Key to Earth's Destiny*. It is repeated here:

"Hail to you, beings of Shan. I greet you in love and peace. My identity is Ashtar, commandant quadra sector, patrol station Schare, all projections, all waves. Greetings. Through the Council of the Seven Lights you have been brought here, inspired with the inner light to help your fellow man. You are mortals, and other mortals can only understand that which their fellow man can understand. The purpose of this organization is, in a sense, to save mankind from himself. Some years ago, your time, your nuclear physicists penetrated the 'Book of Knowledge.' They discovered how to explode the atom. Disgusting as the results have been, that this force should be used for destruction, it not compared to that which can be. We have *not* been concerned with their explosion of plutonium and U235.

"We are concerned, however, with their attempt to explode the hydrogen element. This element is *life giving*, along with five other elements in the air you breathe, in the water you drink, in the composition of your physical self. In much of your material planet is this *life giving* atomic substance, hydrogen. Their efforts in this field of science have been successful to the extent that they are not content to rest on the laurels of a power beyond their use; not content with the entire destruction of an entire city at a time. They must have something more destructive. They've got it. When they explode the hydrogen atom, they shall extinguish life on this planet. They are *tinkering with a formula they do not comprehend*. They are destroying a life-giving element of the Creative Intelligence. Our message to you is this: You shall advance to your government all information we have transmitted to you. You shall request that your government shall immediately contact all other earth nations, regardless of political feelings. Many of your physicists with an inner perception development have refused to have anything to do with the explosion of the hydrogen atom. The explosion of an atom of *inert* substance and that of a *living* substance are two different things. We are not concerned with man's desire to continue war on this planet, Shan. We are concerned with their deliberate determination to *extinguish humanity* and turn this planet into a cinder.

"Your materialists will disagree with our attempt to warn mankind. Rest assured they shall cease to explode *life-giving* atoms, or we shall eliminate all projects connected with such. Our missions are peaceful, but this condition occurred before in this solar system and the planet Lucifer was torn to bits. We are determined that it shall not happen again. The governments on the planet Shan have conceded that we are of a higher intelligence. *They must concede also that we are of a higher authority.* We do not have to enter their buildings to know what they are doing. We have the formula they would like to use. It is not meant for destruction. Your purpose here has been to build a receptivity that we could communicate with your planet, for by

41

the attraction of light substance atoms, we patrol your universe.

"To your government and to your people and through them to all governments and all peoples on the planet of Shan, accept the warning as a blessing that mankind may survive. My light, we shall remain in touch here at this cone of receptivity. My love, I am Ashtar."

As this passage of the manuscript was prepared, Commander Ashtar had fine things to say concerning his former messenger:

"His love for me and his loyalty to our mission was deeply appreciated. He is now a great and busy personage in these realms, continuing tirelessly for the cause of the advancement of knowledge and its eventual application in the New Age. At that time he will be very active in earth's technology advancements and also as a statesman. He now participates in the great universal Councils as a respected elder brother of all people. His placement in your dimension as our spokesman was ordained before his incarnation manifested. His work, combined with the few important others at that point in time, formed the foundation of all that would come later, and nothing shall prevail against the truth as it was expressed at that time."

● ● ●

Surely a close second to the van Tassel contact was Mrs. Ethel P. Hill. Her messages from Ashtar have been lovingly preserved for us in a small book published by Saucerian Publications, of Clarksburg, West Virginia, called *In Days to Come*.

Ethel P. Hill was the wife of an orthodox minister who believed not in any extra-terrestrial communication, and so E.P.H. (who has now passed to the Higher Realm) had need of secret communicative sessions with the Ashtar Command. It is stated that Mrs. Hill was encountered by Ashtar at an airport and requested to become his messenger. These messages were quietly distributed among chosen friends, re-published by the Heralds of the New Age in New Zealand, and finally, edited and prepared for publication by Gray Barker.

Many of her communications from Ashtar are scattered throughout this manuscript, without which this volume would be incomplete.

• • •

Although it happened in the early sixties, to this day Adele Darrah Foley remembers her visit from Ashtar clearly and distinctly. She described that moment in a letter to Marian Hartill a few years later:

"This all happened several years ago, and telling it appears so simple. I only know the whole incident was engraved upon my mind so that every detail of the man who said he was ASHTAR is as fresh as ever.

"I went to sleep one night and then found myself downstairs in the living room. There, standing in front of the fireplace, was a man. He was very tall and slim. His bearing was erect. His hands were clasped behind his back, his feet were slightly apart. He was wearing a light uniform with a high collar. Around the neck was a trim-like braiding which was slightly darker in color. The trim extended down the front. There were no buttons, fastenings, or belt.

"His face was oval, the skin alive, the hair had a definite widow's peak. There was no part. His eyebrows were slim and delicate, the nose was thin, the mouth was rather straight, the lips thin. His eyes were brilliant and penetrating, almond-shaped with a slight oriental appearance.

"I stood waiting while his gaze held me. His expression was very serious and solemn. Then I said, 'How do you do? My name is Adele Darrah.'

"Then he smiled—his teeth were very even and white. It was not a wide smile; little laugh lines appeared at the corner of his eyes. He was very much amused, as he said, 'I know.'

"Then he straightened up and said, with military precision, 'I AM ASHTAR.'

43

"Then everything faded from my memory. I have no idea or memory of what followed. I woke up the next morning only with this memory impressed upon me. I mentioned and described the incident to family and a few friends.

"Later I learned that there *was* an individual named Ashtar. I read the book, *In Days to Come*. Then a little over a year ago a friend told me that two men who had seen Ashtar described him as I did.

"My interest was renewed, and since then I have followed every clue concerning ASHTAR."

• • •

Under the name of "Heralds of the New Age," a small group of New Zealanders attended regular weekly meetings. Their mission was to spread the Good News of the Kingdom of God on earth. They broadly distributed their transmissions, along with those of others, including Mrs. Hill's, throughout the world. Ashtar was a spokesman to this group. Two of these messages follow, typical of many transmissions:

The Vastness of the Universe
By Ashtar

"I would tell you now, dear children, of the many wondrous worlds that are in the universes, for so wondrous are they that your world of Shan is but as nothing. You are trailing around with the sun, as you call it, which is but one of the smaller stars in the heavens. So far distant are many of the stars of even your own universe, that their light takes 300,000 years to come to you!

"As you know, the light from your sun takes but eight minutes to come to you and the light from your moon takes a second and a quarter. If you could but conceive the distance from which the light takes 300,000 years to come! Going around them in orbits greater and smaller are many planets where there dwell beings often as you, yourselves. And these are only in your own

44

universe! Beyond these are many universes greater and more wonderful than that which is your own!

"Can you, my friends, conceive of these things? How great is the Almighty who created all these wondrous places, planets and suns! How worthy of prayer! How worthy of light! How worthy of all adulation from you who dwell on your small planet called Shan! Can you imagine the power and the glory of Him Who made all things, when you realize that the light of the star nearest to your sun takes at least 4-1/2 years to reach you? I, my dear children, pray and worship the Almighty. He is all of all! He is the most important of all things, yet He has given to each of you a spark of Himself. How wonderful! How desirable it is that you should make this spark that He has given to you evolve to such a wondrous extent that it can eventually be taken again to that Eternal Light.

"Your sun, as you know, is of great heat and of great power, and the electricity which comes forth from it is very great. The rays that come to you could be injurious, but the Almighty surrounded your planet with a wonderful envelope which you call an 'atmosphere,' so that the dangerous rays could not pass through.

"As you, my children, know and as we have before informed you, there are many things which you must learn before you advance forward and can build for yourselves those forms which you call space ships. The knowledge will be given to you when you are sufficiently developed for your brains to absorb such wondrous knowledge, and, my dear ones, when all again is peace upon your world. Then will be given to you the plan of that vehicle which you will build so that you may wander forth into the greater places."

The Projection of the Spirit and the Opening of the Third Eye
By Ashtar

"Concerning 'Yoga,' this is merely a way of getting into

touch with the higher forces as you, my dear children, try to do when, in your meditation, you uplift yourselves into that place of light so that you can lose all thought of the physical body. If you could place yourselves intelligently into that sphere, then you would not be at all concerned about that which might be done to your physical body because you would have arisen from the physical up into the mental plane. Yoga is a form of self-hypnotism and those who practice it can hypnotize themselves so that they are not conscious of the physical body in the least and can send forth their spiritual or mental body to other places, not only on your world, but also up into the spiritual realms.

"But you who are of the northern clime, although now you dwell in this your country of New Zealand, have as your Leader, One Who is great and, if you would follow that One, you would not go far amiss. The wonderful stories of this Great One, the Master Jesus, that have been unfolded to you on the knees of your mothers, are of great elevation and will bring you thoughts of a higher kind. You will then enlarge on these things and come eventually to dwell in the spirit where you will meet your Leader; *for all who come to the spiritual realm meet the leaders of their different religions, as you call them. All these religions lead upward to the Throne of the Almighty God, but by different roads.* Elevation of the spirit is what is required, and it matters not by which road a man travels, for on this track, he will go upward to the Divine, the Eternal Father, with whom all will dwell and become as one; for there is no difference in the greater knowledge of the Eternal Spirit. To that he then will go, although he knows not of these things.

"O dear ones, you whom I have been with for many moons, you whom I love, I would take you with me to these realms of beauty where you may dwell eternally in the knowledge and that beauty of spirit, in the radiance that comes from the Eternal source of all. O, you who would bathe yourselves in this knowledge, come with me and let me show you the way to that Eternal One, for know you not that you are one with God? You belong to Him and you must purge yourselves of all that which will soil that beauteous spirit which has been lent to you. O come with me, dear children of Shan, and see those many things which you so desire and those things which you wish to gain knowledge of. If you will, you will find that your elevation will be very great and the beauty of life and that joy which you can experience even in your present form (that one which is of the flesh) will be great. But with selfishness and disparity of spirit you cannot ascend into that realm of eternal life. Give forth to your fellow men, for nothing else matters, for you are all brethren and dwell together upon your world and with you are many from these myriad worlds that are in God's control. If you would know of these things, you need but to raise your mentality into these higher realms so as to put your minds forward and open your 'third eye,' which is so desirable. The third eye, or pineal gland, is of much account to you all, but unfortunately you have lost the use of it in that degrading materialism in which you have dwelt for many centuries.

"O lift yourselves, dear children of Shan, and discern these things, for around you dwell many unseen witnesses. They surround you. If you would but lift your senses and open in the right way, then you would see the many who surround you—those holy spirits who have you in their keeping and would take you to their charge."

• • •

Ashtar first contacted Marian Hartill in the early sixties and continued to do so for about nine years, giving what he said was a "basis for understanding things to come." Some of Marian's material was published by Riley Crabb, of the Borderland Research group in Vista, California.

When the coming of Ashtar was pre-announced to her, he was described as a Commander of all the UFO forces, not a spirit, but an Etherian. Her guides told her he had never been on earth in physical embodiment, that he travels in a body of Light. She was told he looked like a spirit, and anyone not aware might think he was (those distinctions would be difficult since both travel in various dimensions). Marian has confided to us here the highlights of Ashtar's messages outlined in her own words:

"Mankind must choose his own pathway; it is his decision to make. He will either join the Christ forces or the dark forces; there is no in-between. Much depends on previous lives, what has been accomplished and the nature of his progress. The pathway is conditional to the lessons learned. Mankind must be informed of coming events. They are going to be required to understand. Whether or not the earth flips upon its axis will be determined by how many of mankind choose to align them- selves with the Christ Forces of Light. If the people of the Light would release the necessary stabilizing energies to help the UFO friends, it would benefit them greatly to receive that energy, rather than having that energy dispersed to the dark forces.

"There is coming a tremendous battle for the minds of men on earth."

Marian writes:

"I asked Ashtar if my ideas as to the difference between Etherians and spirit people was as I felt it to be."

Ashtar: "Correct, you are correct, we are a form beyond the spirit. I am not saying that these fine Guides and Teachers you have are not wonderful, but we are apart from them, and we are not bound by the same laws that bind them. One day they, too, will have no binding ties to earth, just as we do not.

"We are here because of the job we have to do on your plane in helping to prepare you and others like you for the days of change ahead of you. This tie must remain; it must be strengthened. We of Space are bound to no one but the Christ, our Lord, Commander of all Light, Wisdom and Love."

48

One of the messages from Ashtar, through Marian Hartill is printed below and called:

Our Only Real Protection against Attack

"I am with you today because I have a warning for you all. I bring not fear. I bring Light and a new awareness of that which is coming into your life, not directly, but indirectly through others you know. You are well aware of the negative nature of man around you; now you must be aware of that negation which is being released through the fourth dimension which will burst forth to confound and confront the mind and body of man upon the third dimension. The masses are not prepared for this in any measure, and it will rest upon your shoulders to bring as much understanding as possible to those you know who will be panic stricken.

"This is not the Lower Astral; this is a far more gruesome aspect of life than that. The knowledge of the Christ-Light and protection it gives is of major importance, as it is the *only real protection a third dimension being has against attack.* Locked doors mean nothing to this rampaging evil, that in itself knows no laws as you do.

"Lester (Marian's guide) has repeatedly told you to practice concentration upon a single point. This is our way of trying to get you to hold the Christ-Light vibration. You all do well in surrounding yourselves and your homes with this Light, but you do not hold it long enough; so that it dissipates from lack of concentrated thought.

"You must at all times feel and radiate *LIGHT,* Christ-Light, to protect yourselves fully. Have it become such a strong part of your make-up that it is instantaneous at all times. Practice, practice, practice. It may mean the difference between Life and death to one you love or are trying to help protect.

"Remember, this is your job and we can only do so much. *Our help is directly balanced with your own effort*—past that we cannot step; so don't be found asleep at the switch.

"This is a *warning* to all whom this message may contact. I speak with *urgency* to all who stand with the Christ Forces in this greatest of all wars."

And from an earlier message in November:

"The lower levels of the astral plane have been swept clean. This cleansing will cause a sharp upswing in crime and perversion of all nature. Confusion and fear shall rule man of earth for being freed from the hold of the lower forces—the mass shall have to rearrange its energy, and it does not by nature know how to or even that a re-balance must take place. Your position in the *LIGHT* is as *secure as your desire is to remain there;* so cling to the Light, and remember that we here are beside you on whatever path you may find yourself tomorrow, or a year from tomorrow, as long as your goal is Spiritual Understanding, and an awareness of the Higher Self. I am Ashtar."

• • •

From the very beginning of his contact with our solar system, Ashtar has continued to expand his areas of communication through countless beautiful spiritual messengers too numerous to mention, even were we aware of them all. We have not intentionally failed to mention any certain ones nor set out to show any favoritism; we have simply worked from the material Ashtar has seen fit to place at our disposal.

The contributions of all of his messengers have been great works left behind in the hands of mankind. Many have come upon the scene, fulfilled their vow to labor with him, and then returned to higher realms to serve creation from that sector. They have come and they have returned. Many still remain. But the words of Ashtar, through them, remain to herald the truth, to lead mankind, to plead the cause of freedom and right, to steady the hand of man's government of himself, his world, his life, his soul.

II
Ashtar And The Mission

The Mission To Planet Earth

The Mission to planet Earth involves millions of souls, within the Intergalactic Fleets or in embodiment. Commander Ashtar is the local Administrator of that broad program.

Many earth-based individuals, working as single units, have wholeheartedly joined in the responsibilities of that Mission in various creative endeavor. Gerald T. Ross, a California broker, is a case in point. He was so deeply moved by the Ashtar Command "Evacuation" book, he prepared the following excellent summary and personally assumed responsibility for its wide distribution. We reprint it here because it so conclusively and adequately summarizes the Mission of the Intergalactic Commands to our planet.

People of Planet Earth:

Your planet is in imminent danger of cataclysmic upheavals because of disruptions in the magnetic field. This is caused by the tremendous negative vibrations you have been transmitting to one another for these thousands of years. The hatred, wars, murder, and atomic experiments have all collectively added extra weight in the form of negative energy to poles of your planet, and very soon it is likely to tilt further on its axis, creating destruction to the surface of your planet through resulting earthquakes, tidal waves, volcanoes, and windstorms of unprecedented velocities.

MOST of the people of earth would be killed—if it were not for us, your space *brothers and sisters* who are monitoring force and danger to you every moment of your existence.

There are *millions,* yes, *millions of space ships invisible* to your eyes at your present level of "vibration." For years we have been encircling your planet; some of our "mother ships" anchored high in your atmosphere are *100 miles across:* These "mother ships" contain entire cities with gardens, grass, trees, and accommodations for literally millions of people!

Why are we telling you this? Because we are on a mission of LOVE from the *ALLIANCE FOR PEACE FROM THE INTERGALACTIC COUNCIL* whose authority comes from the *SPIRITUAL HIERARCHY OF THE SOLAR SYSTEM,* whose Supreme Commander is *JESUS CHRIST—SANANDA,* he is called by us of the Alliance.

You see, people of Earth, we represent a great confederation of planets, all of whom have long given up war as a solution to problems. Because we are of a great number, you get conflicting accounts of our descriptions when your people see us. We are many of a spiritual design and come from a different dimension. This is one reason we are invisible to you.

Another reason is, we do not wish to *FRIGHTEN YOU IN ANY WAY.* Ours is a *MISSION OF LOVE.* We could have long ago easily subdued you and made you slaves, if that had been our desire. Our technology is "awesome."

We, *The Alliance for Peace* from the Intergalactic Council are *forbidden* to interfere in the affairs of the souls of any planet and their evolution *without the approval of the government(s)* of that planet. The *penalty* for unauthorized interference is immediate annihilation of the interfering species. The only *exception* is, when the *LAWS OF THE UNIVERSE* are violated, we may interfere with the other members of the universe. Such an example is atomic war. We simply will not permit it except on a very limited basis, because we know it not only kills the physical body, but also *damages the soul* and inflicts tremendous trauma to that soul, requiring a great deal of repair. Atomic war is one of the three cataclysms which will trigger your evacuation from the planet earth!

We have, on many occasions, revealed ourselves to various individuals on the planet earth. In fact, we have *thousands* of representatives walking, working, and living among you *now!* You may recognize them by their tremendously serene personalities when you are in their presence. They are sons and daughters, sisters and brothers of the Light.

We have attempted to convince your government(s) (oh yes, they know of us!) that *we come in peace* and wish to lift you above your present level of evolution through the vast technology we want to give you. However, we have been met with *hostility* and *suspicion.* Even now, your movies and television shows depict all space beings as being *hostile,* bent on subjugating you to slavery—or worse—and having a greatly different appearance than yours.

The truth is, *most of us look and are just like you in appearance. Most of us evolved from the same source* eons and eons past. However, unlike you people of Earth, we learned to live peacefully, and to direct our energy and technology outward into the universe in a spirit of *Brotherhood of Man.*

You see, our technology is based upon the natural physical laws of the universe, which includes the Light which flows out from the Creator God and the energy of magnetism.

Because of our knowledge of universal law, our very being consists of a higher level of "vibration" than you people of Earth. You see, every particle of the universe consists of molecules whose center contains an atom around which electrons and protons revolve. Each molecule of a different molecular structure "vibrates" at a different frequency. The inside of a molecule is identical in makeup to the universe. Planets revolve around central suns; solar systems, around galaxies; galaxies, around a central sun. Each molecule "vibrates" at whatever frequency seems appropriate for our existence.

As one *becomes more spiritual* in nature, thinking only of the welfare of others and not of power and greed, the higher the molecules of his being will vibrate. As we know in our dimension, it is possible for these molecules to vibrate so rapidly that the frequency becomes pure light. This is why we call ourselves the FORCES OF LIGHT. We depend on the light from THE SOURCE—THE CREATOR, GOD, for our existence.

We will dwell just a moment on the *Forces of Darkness.* These are beings from the lower realms we refer to as the *Destroyer.* They are to be avoided. It is these forces which inspire hatred, murder, war, lust, greed and all other aspects of the lower nature. Aspire yourselves to walk in the Light. Be alert to psychic attacks from these beings.

We have come to fulfill the destiny of this planet, which is to experience a short period of "cleansing" and then to usher in a NEW GOLDEN AGE OF LIGHT.

We are here to lift off the *surface,* yes *and inner world,* during this period of cleansing, those *souls who are walking in the Light* on the Earth.

As mentioned before, the *souls of Light* are you people of Earth who have lived according to universal truths and have put the concerns of others before your own; you who have put aside personal greed, lust for power, aspirations of wealth "at all costs." Souls of Light are you who recognize GOD as the SOURCE OF ALL THAT IS GOOD.

The short period of cleansing the planet is IMMINENT— EVEN THE MIDNIGHT HOUR!

We have *millions* of space ships stationed in the skies above your planet, ready to instantly lift you off at the first warning of your planet's beginning to *tilt on its axis.* When this happens, we have only a *very short time* in which to lift you from the surface before *great tidal waves* will lash your coast-lines—possibly five miles or more high! They will cover much of your land masses!

These tidal waves will unleash great earthquakes and volcanic eruptions and cause your continents to split and sink in places and cause others to rise.

We are *very experienced* in the evacuation of populations of planets! *This is nothing new for the galactic fleet!* We expect to complete the evacuation on Earth of the souls of Light in 15 minutes—even though they are of a tremendous number.

We shall rescue the souls of Light first. On our great galactic computers we have stored every thought, every act you have done in this and previous lifetimes. Our computers are locked onto the coordinates where you Souls of Light are located. At the *first* indication of need to evacuate, our computers will lock onto the location of the Souls of Light where they are at that instant!

After the souls of Light have been evacuated, then the *children* will be lifted off. The children are not old enough to be accountable, so they will be evacuated to special ships to be cared for until they can be reunited with their parents. There will be people specially trained to handle their trauma. Many may be put to sleep for awhile to help them overcome their fear and anxiety. Our computers are so sophisticated—far beyond anything ever used on Earth in this age—and can locate mothers and fathers of children wherever they are and notify them of their safety. *Make no mistake, your children shall be lifted to safety during the evacuation!*

After the evacuation of the children, the invitation will be extended to all remaining souls on the planet to join us. However, this will be for only a *very short time—perhaps only 15 minutes.* There is no question of having *enough space on board the ships for you,* but because the atmosphere by this time will be full of fire, flying debris, poisonous smoke, and because the magnetic field of your planet will be disturbed, we will have to leave your atmosphere very quickly or we, also, with our space ships, would perish.

Therefore, he who steps into our levitation beams first will be lifted first. Any hesitation on your part would mean the end of your third dimensional existence you call the physical body.

Which brings us to the most serious and difficult part of the evacuation: As mentioned earlier, souls of Light have a *higher vibration* frequency than those who are more closely "tied" to the earth and its ways.

Since our levitation beams which will be lifting you off the surface of this planet are *very close to the same thing as your electrical charges, those of low vibrational frequency* may not be able to withstand the *high* frequency of the levitation beams without departing their third-dimensional bodies. If this happens, then your soul will be released to join our God, the Father. "In His house are many mansions."

If you do not decide to step into the levitation beams to be lifted up, you might be one of the few who survive the "cleansing" of the planet for the *NEW GOLDEN AGE*. However, during this period of cleansing, there will be great changes in climate, changes in land masses, as the poles of the planet will have a *new orientation*. This alone will create untold hardship for the survivors who may still not make it to the New Age.

The most important point for you to remember is this:

Any show of fear lowers your frequency of vibration, thus making you less compatible with our levitation beams!!

Therefore:

Above all else, REMAIN CALM. DO NOT PANIC. Know that you are in expert hands, hands which have extensive experience in evacuation of ENTIRE PLANETS!

WE CANNOT OVEREMPHASIZE THIS: REMAIN CALM! RELAX! DO NOT PANIC WHEN YOU STEP INTO OUR LEVITATION BEAMS.

What is to happen to you if you survive the lift off? First you will be taxied to our "mother ships" anchored high above the planet where you will be taken care of during your great trauma. Some of you may need medical attention. Our expert medical staff will be there to treat you with our highly advanced medical equipment. You will be fed and housed until such time as transfer elsewhere is advisable.

Some of you will be taken to cities on other planets to be trained in our advanced technology *before being returned to the planet earth to start the New Golden Age.*

Your beautiful planet earth is destined to be the most beautiful star in the universe. A planet of Light! Here, you will rejoin the remainder of the Universe in *brotherly love and fellowship with God the Father.*

People of Earth: We love you! Do not scoff at these words. As surely as the sun shines from the east to the west, so shall these things shortly come to pass!

The cataclysms will begin *without warning!* Everything will happen so fast, you will not have time to think! Think on these things *now!*

Think; picture yourself standing with all the havoc around you; people screaming and running; others on their knees praying; automobiles crashing; glass breaking; buildings falling; ground shaking and gaping with huge cracks; debris falling all around you!

Think NOW.' What shall I do? Answer: RE-MAIN CALM and WITHOUT FEAR. Maintain an inner peace of mind and STEP INTO THE LEVI-TATION BEAMS which flow from the underneath center of our space craft.

As you are informed now as to what to do, SPREAD THE WORD to everyone you know. *BE FAITHFUL TO GOD! THE TIME IS VERY SHORT!* Perhaps we shall no longer be able to restrain the tilt of the earth's axis,' as we have been able to do with our energy beams and transmitters for the past several years.

There is still a chance—a slight chance, that this great upheaval can be avoided. However, it will take extreme coop-

eration from you people of Earth—cooperation unlike you have ever exhibited before in this age.

1. Avoid giving off negative energy through your distrust, greed, hatred and begin to help each other. By helping each other, you give off positive vibrations (energy). *LOVE GOD.* The positive energy in large mass will neutralize the weight of negative energy which has built up around the pole of your planet—this could keep it from tilting if enough positive energy is received in time. Your planet is a living organism. Send mental positive energy by thanking the earth for all its bountifulness you have received.

2. By whatever *peaceful* means at your disposal put sufficient pressure on your government(s) to permit us to land our spaceships on your planet and meet with your leaders and offer them our assistance and technology. *WE WILL NOT DO THIS UNTIL WE ARE ASSURED WE WILL NOT BE TREATED WITH HOSTILITY OR BE INCARCERATED.* With the cooperation of your world governments, we can greatly help you in more orderly evacuation of your planet, if indeed it still becomes necessary—*WHICH IT MAY!*

WE HOPE YOU WILL TAKE THESE WORDS ON FAITH, BUT IF NOT, DO RESEARCH AND PROVE THEM TO BE TRUE FOR YOURSELVES. MEDITATE DAILY AND YOU WILL FIND AND KNOW THE TRUTH. PEACE BE WITH YOU.

• • •

The work of Mr. Ross and hundreds like him so beautifully illustrates the spirit of personal involvement captured by Ashtar when he created the Command banner shown earlier in this volume. It is designed to be a focus of inspiration wherever it is placed. As we look upon it, we realize that each one of us is also a part of the Great Mission. As individuals we are guarding the Light, wherever we are; as we live in Love, Love is in action wherever we are, emanating a frequency of cooperation with our sacrificing Space Friends, allied with them in our dedication to the Kingdom of God on Earth.

Thinking upon the words of the banner will create a mind to mind link on inner levels of consciousness with the Guardians of Terra. As we repeat it aloud daily, we reinforce our fellowship with our Space Friends and magnetize their Light to us.

The logo design, in the banner center, suggested by Ashtar, contains two symbolical colors—the deep Universal Blue on a White field, encompassing the Great White Light of God. It is surrounded by two circles which, combined, represent all earth-based volunteers of Light. The inner circle within the circle denotes the Intergalactic Legion of Special Volunteers. The great winged "A" symbolizes all of the Commands as the airborne division of the Brotherhood of Light. The small scout ship, or shuttle craft, is to remind us of the constant alert and preparation for instant evacuation if and when that becomes necessary.

Therefore, in a sense the logo of Ashtar is itself a symbol of the Mission to Planet Earth.

Administering The Program

"As Commander for this solar system and its various volunteer units from many areas of space, it is my responsibility to coordinate these efforts of the many fleets as they touch into the mission to planet Earth. When these various factions of force are not thus involved, then of course, they are self-regulatory and guided under their own supervision. They only come under the jurisdiction of the Interplanetary Confederation if they are here on a specific assignment, correlated to the overall Hierarchical mission to the planet.

"Many there are who come simply of their own volition and their own purposes. To these, we merely extend our hospitality and our accord. The exception to that rule would be any of those who come for reasons that would be harmful to the planet or its inhabitants. These we carefully police, and escort beyond the system on their way.

"From other worlds there are often replacement fleets who come to relieve others of their tour of duty. There is a continuing turnover of fleet participation in the many patrol units involved. Those tours of duty are not of an indefinite nature, but have a set period to begin and to end, with others coming forth to replace them. There is a set time of relief from duty, when those replaced will return. The assignment given to these many volunteer fleets is done on a 'need-of-the-moment' basis.

"Strong representative ground units necessitate contacts in keeping with the frequencies of the fleet and its representative. Thus one representative will primarily always be in contact

61

with its own Interstellar Command, even though the crew may be replaced occasionally, but always by their own members.

"There are other earth-based personnel who are representatives 'at large,' who may make contact and be at the disposal of any Command units in the area. However, do remember that each base or earth unit does, at all times, have its personal *craft hovering within its vortex for personal immediate relay of messages to or from that unit.* This station or platform never changes, although the persons involved might be removed temporarily for rest and relaxation, to return later. All of our signals, beams, and contacts are relayed to our messengers through the medium of these individual platforms of contact. You, Tuella, have experienced a few times of speaking with these station personnel, but customarily they do not personally enter into the communication themselves. The relocation of a based unit will also imply the like relocation of its relay station. The personal vortex follows the based unit.

"In the atmosphere above a base unit, there is an identifying beam that projects incredibly high above it for identification purposes to those who patrol by. This beam projection identifies the particular command sponsoring the base unit.

"Those of you who serve in your places, be assured that all who participate in this program know you are there! It is beautiful to behold these beams of Light, as one looks down upon the planet from our ships high above you in orbit. A similar projection also is in evidence in locations of intense Light activity, such as meetings, seminars, etc.

"True, the planet has a distinct morbid darkness about it due to its layered negativity clouds, but nevertheless, these beautiful light beams penetrate that darkness with a ray that thrills our hearts!

"Beyond the vicinity of our local solar system there is the entire galaxy containing the remaining solar systems. All of these in representation represent the Galactic Commands, who join forces with our Local Spiritual Hierarchy in its program for the betterment of Earth. Thus we have the Ashtar Command, which is the official Command of our solar system. Then we have, as well, the assistance of the Commands from the rest of our own galaxy. These enter into a full cooperation for monitoring the planet.

"When, as Commander, I am in need of further assistance for any kind of emergency, I can then reach beyond the Galactic Command to the Intergalactic Federation of Free Worlds for greater Interstellar representation locally. This brings into the patrol effort, millions more men and craft to participate in any crisis.

"This larger representative group, when entering the area of our solar system, is placed at the disposal of and under the jurisdiction of our Ashtar Command, in expediting assignments. The spirit of cooperation which is present in all of these interchanges of assistance is one the planet Earth could well use as a pattern. Thus we have not only the entire galaxy, but many other galaxies and representation of the universe. There are also certain and specific fleets and volunteers who come even from other universes, other constellations, to wholeheartedly join in our efforts locally.

"This tremendous participation is the result of the broad and scattered Tribunals, on a universal level, a galactic level, and solar system levels. All levels of life throughout the omniverse are represented at these great Councils. Sometimes it seems to me personally that there is time for little else but Council attendance, but I am the Space Council member representing our own solar system at all of these great Tribunals. At these tremendous sessions, the problems of all are discussed as well as the relationship of the problems of others to ourselves. The entire omniverse is informed and alert concerning the great danger to the other systems posed by Earth's indelicate participation in nuclear physics as a tool of war. The development of the hydrogen bomb within our local solar system brought immediate widespread cooperation between galaxies and Universal Councils to monitor the situation. The Ashtar Command, being local to the threat, was given the responsibility of coordinating this monitoring and attempting to educate the Eartheans of the need to attain a higher frequency of love for one another, as well as developing in Interstellar rapport with other systems.

"As a part of this tremendous program, thousands of units were earth based on the planet as a point of contact and for liaison reports. This has been the mission, and splendid cooperation from all dimensions of Space has increased the effectiveness of the program.

"The forthcoming events, as they begin to unfold inevitably, will bring many more participants from other dimensions than are presently active. However, all participants do remain in a state of alert and readiness for that call to come. All know of the global situation, the pressures in international affairs, and the pressures upon and within the planet itself. There is a readiness throughout the universe that inspires me in my responsibility as Director of the Program. I know that they will not fail in their moment of summons to the present ranks.

"These various systems and constellations of many planets from other galaxies do, as a part of their commitment to the Light, have their earth-based representatives who monitor the earth situation at very close range through infiltration. They also report back to their liaison centers the result of their observations. These representatives of other distant forces do also have their embodied contacts present upon the scene. The bringing together of these two factors becomes your reported physical contactee experiences, which excite so much interest throughout the UFO circles. Each segment of the volunteer fleets does each have its own earth-based contacts as well as positioned representatives, yet there is a magnificent smoothness of cooperation through them all. The Program of Light for Planet Earth is a well coordinated interlocking effort from multitudes of sectors of Outer Space. When the danger has passed and the earth has been renewed in its restoration and functions as a participating unit of its own solar system, then the combined program will change to one of instruction and education, through intermingling Intergalactic fellowship, cultural exchange, and interdimensional access and travel. Instead of a United Nations as you presently have, there will be a Federation of United Worlds, living in peace and trade interchange. Instead of groping for a One World attitude, as is presently the case, there will be an accepted concept of One Universe. These are the great concepts the forces of darkness seek to destroy, and will use all of their power to prevent this ultimate realization of Love between worlds. But their efforts shall fail! When this concept of One Universe is known and a successfully working principle, then we can truly say, *mission completed.*

"In the meantime, we concentrate upon our own solar system and its needs for a successfully working program for peace. Only Earth remains outside of this program within our family of planets, but soon that shall be rectified and this, our solar system, will take its united place in our galactic affairs. This will be a great victory for this sector of Space. To this end, all of us join our efforts of Love, our technologies, our statesmanship, and our disbursement of information, to realize the goal of *PEACE ON EARTH, GOOD WILL TOWARD MEN.*

"There will be an interval of time in which the planet will need to rest from its chaotic adjustment, in preparation for its coming galactic representation. During this period, following its cleansing and its revolt against the dark ones, the planet will be permitted a period of rest and quietness, until it becomes habitable again. During this inaction the saints of God and the Light representatives will be the guests of this galaxy in many different locations, while awaiting their return to earth again. They will be fully instructed concerning the future in store for Earth and its participation in Intergalactic life. They will be knowledgeable and trained in the new form of government and the proper supervision of planetary affairs. They will be given earth-based members of other worlds to abide with men for as long as it is necessary, to launch their new life as a planet of Light and Love. When Earth has healed itself of all of its tribulations, a New Age of Enlightenment will begin for those who return for its mission of restoration. *THIS IS THE PROGRAM, THIS IS THE PLAN, AND IT SHALL NOT FAIL!* I am Ashtar."

THE UNIVERSAL GOVERNING SYSTEM

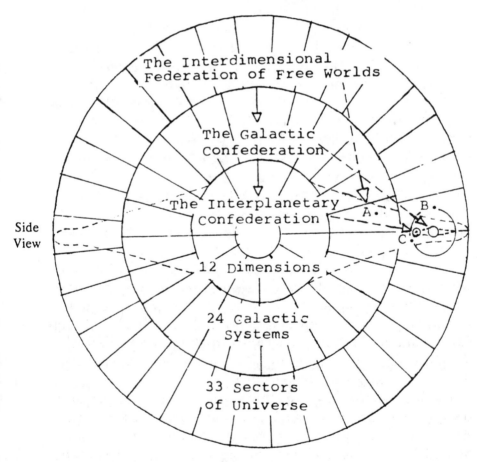

A. Universe
B. Galaxy
C. Solar system (Local)

The Interdimensional Alliance

From Oscar Magocsi, Canadian channel for the interdimensional Federation (the particular group represented in the message called themselves the "Luminarians"), we have a very good outline of the various divisions of Outer Space forces:

"We are all a part of the great multiverse, or cosmos of Creation. All help one another. It is an Alliance, but no one is permitted to direct another's affairs, only to assist. Tremendous restructuring has been going on, working toward a more standardized mode of communication, procedures, even manufactured items, to form an interchangeable system for all worlds, making it possible to have a more efficient Alliance. Efficiency of organization is only possible through standardization.

"*THE INTERPLANETARY CONFEDERATION,* which is under the Command of Ashtar within your solar system, is the one responsible for planet Earth, within your star system only. The Ashtar Command is linked with the Galactic Confederation. They use many fleets from the larger *FEDERATION,* which are standing by. These are under Ashtar's jurisdiction for any evacuation emergency.

"Your planets have separate spiritual hierarchies of their own, besides the overall hierarchy for the entire solar system. All are tied inexplicably with the Master Jesus Sananda. Should the need arise, Ashtar can also call upon the Galactic Fleets for support.

"*THE GALACTIC CONFEDERATION* is no more than four parts of the Interdimensional Federation of Free Worlds. It means the Galactic Confederation of the Milky Way Galaxy. They willingly lend out much necessary support to the Ashtar Command, and if more resources are needed, they can draw upon the vast resources of the Interdimensional Federation. This is happening all of the time. It also explains why one Space source may not actually be familiar with another, or possibly never heard the name. We are speaking of millions of personnel and craft from far flung distant Space.

"*THE INTERDIMENSIONAL FEDERATION OF FREE WORLDS* is the larger body, being made up of thirty-three vast sectors in an all-encompassing body. It is simplified simply to speak of the *FEDERATION,* for we are from everywhere in the Cosmos, which is vaster and far greater. Thus when one refers to the *FEDERATION,* the *INTERDIMENSIONAL FEDERATION OF FREE WORLDS* is meant by that term.

"To clarify this organization, think of this: You live in a big city (solar system) and you have a municipal government (Ashtar Command) looking after the affairs of your city. Now, besides the municipal government your city happens to be within a province or state of the union (Galactic Confederation). Now aside from that, all the states and cities are within the federal system (Interdimensional Federation) as well. In your world a federal government can overrule decisions of state, or municipal governments, but in the Cosmic Scheme of things that is not so. They are all interrelated but not necessarily subjugated. They are side by side allies, like good neighbors.

"Another analogy would be that your star system happens to be one of many farms (solar systems) in the state (galaxy), and/or the whole area. The farmers association (Confederation) is willing to help out an individual farmer with whatever he needs in case of problems. But, they cannot issue direct orders or directives to that individual farmer no matter what the case. The farmer will have to decide whatever is good for his own farm. Now the association may advise, or suggest, but they cannot enforce.

"This is the same thing. It is analogous to Ashtar's being your farmer and the Confederation's being the association of farmers. Between friends and neighbors or a vast community of farmers, *there is no such thing as a chain of command.*

"It is possible to have a military structure on a smaller scale, but on a large scale it is not possible to do such things; it is far too vast. In other words, the only way that it could be done is according to voluntary contribution. It is possible that they (Ashtar Command) can set up a chain of command amongst themselves because they are only looking after this relatively smaller one star system and they can rely on the support of the Galactic Confederation. The Galactic Confederation can have a certain amount of standardization; however, even they do not have a perfectly full standardization from one end to the other. They are a part of too many diverse systems, cultures, technologies, and procedures.

"Most worlds are not even willing to adopt the ways of other worlds. Why would they? They have perfectly well functioning space travel and technologies. So therefore, we are faced with a rather strange problem. We are unified in spirit, but are far from being perfectly standardized in communications, practices, or transportation systems, on either a Confederation or Federation scale.

"It is customary in every system, including your planet Earth, to send an independent observer and field agent. Many are Planetary Directors for the Federation, who are really more like Intergalactic Diplomats. Each has to do his own task, just as any earth Ambassador would do. Each has to do his independent reporting to the Federation, which naturally involves some duplication of these things through the Ashtar Command and the Confederation. There is enough coverage done that every important issue is thoroughly covered and reported. The Federation could also learn through the Ashtar Command sources or the Confederation.

"These earth-based unit Commanders have their guidelines, given in briefing, on how to do certain things, but other than that, their own discretion is used when on the field. Generally speaking, they have statutes and three assistant representatives. There is an agreed-upon procedure, a give and take, with some overlapping areas. The field agent assumes full responsibility to do their best within the guidelines. When a problem is beyond them, they may contact an advisory board at base for clarification.

"If it is anything to do with security measures, Ashtar is immediately notified, for the Ashtar Command watches over the local solar system. It is their responsibility and they are present there to accomplish it. In security matters, clarification is made, but where evacuation plans are concerned, they are totally through Ashtar's discretion. Every issue of importance has to be consulted upon and confirmed by the Confederation under the Command of Ashtar."

• • •

Through the very fine messengership of Gladys Rodehaver of El Paso, Texas, we have further words from Ashtar discussing his Command. (The message was sent to us by a friend).

"There are millions of craft operating in this solar system at all times and many, many of these belong to the Ashtar Command. Some are stationed far above your planet and are more or less stationary for long periods of time, keeping track of the earth on their monitoring systems. Others move about, discharging their various duties. We have small craft doing surveying activities and we have larger craft with extended range that are capable of operating in space and which visit planets in other solar systems.

"We also have what you know as 'mother ships' or 'mother craft,' with many, many smaller craft coming and going from the mother ship. There is a great deal of activity in what earthlings think of as empty space. We are capable of invisibility and when our craft are traveling beyond the speed of light, we do become invisible to the physical eye.

"Our purpose is service, and we go where we are needed anywhere in this sector. Our headquarters is on one of the largest of the mother craft, and orders and instructions come from this craft. It is a city in itself. Most of our people are natives of *one or another of the planets in this solar system,* but also we do have those working with us from other solar systems. Our workers do visit their home planets at various times on what you might call vacations. Most of us have worked together for a very long time; we are a well-knit Confederation and feel that we are an effective one.

"I will leave you now in the Light of the Creator. I am Ashtar. Adonai."

• • •

Commander Korton gave me this brief discussion concerning the heavenly organizations:

"It is well to anchor the truth of the heavenly groups within Earth's hemispheres to help persons of Light to understand the Etherical patrols and to properly assess the guardians. Those of other universes are not forbidden to come. Earth souls need some source of evaluation to exercise and measure their own discernment.

"The Ashtar Command of this hemisphere embodies all of the lesser Commands that are a working volunteer portion of those aligned with the Great Brotherhood of Light to lift the vibrations of planet Earth, hopefully to prevent disastrous action and calamities which might destroy it and interfere with the galaxy as well.

"Now let us consider the situation that prevails for the present in the organization of the heavenly forces. We have 592 different Commands formerly of the local Planetary Confederation for Interplanetary Peace, that are now joined in unison with the Alliance of Planets now known as the *INTERDIMENSIONAL FEDERATION* which forms the great Intergalactic Council. Your own Saturnian Tribunal is representative of this solar system, while the Intergalactic Council is representative of the Universe. We remain and work for service to Earth within this Universe alone, as do you.

"However, there are millions of other worlds within other universes representing untold galaxies, who also traverse the heavens and weave in and out of solar systems, usually on exploratory and fact finding missions for their own universities and laboratories or scientific experiments. These also represent many contactors with persons on your planet. It is not unwise for souls to learn of these many sources, their purpose and the fact that many of these would not even be aware of the personnel of our local Commands and Forces. Likewise, very many of these are also unknown to me and my comrades. This is a point worth remembering. This is Korton, closing transmission."

• • •

In the highly respected Bob Renaud material (originally presented by Gabriel Green in Flying Saucers International*), part 15 of Issue 19 contains a fantastic report of the Third Conclave of Elder Masters, held on Arcturia. Master Kren Lor was speaking concerning the History of the United Galaxy and Alliance:*

"The tremendous organization now known as United Galaxy Alliance, is also called the *UNITED WORLD ALLIANCE,* the *ALL WORLDS FEDERATION,* and the *GALACTIC UNISON.*"

In the context, however, the conclave is usually simply referred to as *THE ALLIANCE* (1962). In my research in our time ('84–'85) I find that the *INTERDIMENSIONAL FED-*

ERATION OF FREE WORLDS (the same Cosmic Council) is most often referred to concisely as the *WORLD FEDERATION,* or even more simply as *THE FEDERATION.*

At the Third Conclave of this elite body (1962), Masters from 5,000 planets were in attendance, including four from our own solar system. You can readily understand why I constantly exhort my fellow Eartheans to "get the big picture!" As we contemplate that "big picture" it is a bit helpful to comprehend the distinction between the Greater Federation, as compared to the Galactic Confederation, and the further distinction of our own local solar system's *ASHTAR COMMAND.* We trust this section of information has been a bit helpful toward that end.

The Beloved "Commander-in-Chief," Jesus the Christ "Ruler of Shan"

I, for one, have been very appreciative of the following words written by Gray Barker as he introduced Mrs. Hill's book:

"There are many who feel that ASHTAR and his legions are the forerunners of the Second Coming of Christ—no matter how this is understood. Some expect to see Him in the flesh; others believe that the Spirit of Christ will eventually rule the earth, and the spiritually 'unfit' will be eliminated. At any rate, many people feel that our so-called culture is nearing its end and that something is about to happen. A change must come both in world affairs and in religion, whose doctrines were fashioned, not by Jesus, but by medieval priests in order to keep the ignorant in spiritual bondage to the Church.

"The Ancient Wisdom ever remains the same, although Truth may be presented in many forms, and in the course of ages may become covered with the barnacles of superstition.

"Great Spiritual Intelligences seek suitable channels to convey spiritual truths, and *at times of crisis there is always an influx of 'messages' from other worlds.*"

It seems to me that one of the most inspiring areas of the character of Ashtar is his consistent and enthusiastic devotion to Jesus the Christ.

I asked him, "What is your relationship to Jesus?" He answered:

"The same as yours. He is a revered and respected great Being of Light proceeding from the government of the Great Central Sun. He is a beloved Teacher through this entire universe, known and loved by all. His sacrifices for the cause of Light are tremendous above that of any other, and for this planet He has truly earned His position of World Teacher. However, He is involved with the entire universe and not simply this planet. His prestige is much more prodigious on other worlds than on this planet, where He has been scorned many times.

"I have served with our Beloved World Teacher, as His assistant and representative through many eons and cultures, particularly upon this planet. When the plans for His Galilean embodiment were finalized, I volunteered my energies to His mission without reservation. The closeness of our relationship has sometimes created a confusion between the two by many sincere souls. That may be explained later in this text.

"Our great craft has patrolled this system for many many ages before our direct contact and accelerated influence began in the 'forties of your time span. The history of our contact with humanity is recorded, but most do not recognize it as such, neither accept it in that light. But in every instance, preserved in sacred writings of contact from another dimension of time and space heralds our presence. Those who received us were in most cases themselves a part of us and the divine Hierarchy, of this System Authority, or planetary Guardians, as you might term them today.

"I was the first appointed to my task of Galactic supervision of extraterrestrial fleets on mission to Earth, and have remained in that service ever since. I am one with the Beloved Commander, and serve with Him and the Heavenly Host in

His Name, and for the benefit of planet Earth and humanity. Our assignment has been long and arduous, but we shall prevail and see the Kingdom of God on Earth. We serve in the interest of Truth, and the Glory of the Radiant One to see God's Divine Plan fulfilled. That is the mission of my life and of all those who serve with me."

And we remember His words of benediction in "The Golden Book":

"The Ashtar Command, and all of my fellow Commanders and the members of all of our fleets, serve in the Light of the Radiant One. Our dedication is to His Great Mission, which is much broader than His Mission to Earth. The scope of His Love and His teachings has penetrated many universes. The Love of the Radiant One is a nucleus and a center, a focus of creation, throughout Infinity. This Love for Him Who is the Light of the World, that fills your heart this beautiful sunrise, is shared by all of the universes."

• • •

Carole Hall, Messenger of Menlo Park, California, also asked this same question and received her answer in a joint statement from Sanut Kumara, Lady Master Venus and Master Aljanon:

Carole: "I ask to know the relationship of Master Jesus and the one known as Ashtar, for the energies of the two seem often to blend together into a combined vibration."

Answer: "The similarity that you sense in the vibrations of these two beings, Ashtar and Jesus, is because of a predominant ray affinity they share as well as a common interplanetary frequency of consciousness, as pertains to the nature of their particular missions.

"The nature of Hierarchal work varies with each planet because of the inherent vibrational patterns of manifestation peculiar to each. Additionally, the linkage to which we referred earlier which bonds each round of evolution on one planet overlaps that of rounds of other planets, some of which have not yet manifested and others which have long ago manifested.

"Earth scientists have called Venus 'Earth's twin planet,' unaware of the cosmic truth which they voice. Herein lies the seed to the answer."

• • •

An example of this blending of vibrations is very evident in Ashtar's message to Mrs. Hill, called A LETTER TO YOU FROM SCHARE.

"We will continue our description of life on Venus, as a fitting prelude to our well earned privilege of serving in our present capacity—not technically designated as 'teachers' but more in the role of 'elder brothers,' guiding, encouraging and commending any forward step, as our comrades of earth fall into line with our steady march toward our goal—the acceptance of our Beloved Commander-in-Chief, Jesus Christ, as Ruler of Shan (planet earth)! Until He mounts His rightful throne of Power and Glory, and is accepted by mankind in a true spirit of loyalty and devotion, we are bound by our sacred word of honor to serve in any way which will speed that denouement.

"Your planet was given a rare opportunity to learn the true and dependable Laws leading to progress along *all* lines of achievement—physical, mental, and spiritual—when the One known to you as Jesus Christ was sent in human embodiment, not only to teach but to demonstrate in full sight of earth dwellers the Beauty, the Efficacy and the Supreme Wisdom of compliance with those powerful Creative Laws enunciated by the Omnipotent Creator of All Things!

"This advent of The Christ occurred at what seems to us a very short time ago and many of us watched with fascinated eyes and the most intense desire and hope, to see this Saviour of mankind accepted and acclaimed Ruler of the Planet Shan by unanimous consent!

"Alas! The failure of all but a mere handful of people to catch even a fleeting glimpse of the sublime spiritual message He brought, which would have freed them from all *bondage* to material things—their complete *BLINDNESS*—filled our hearts with sorrowful despair of any possible chance for Shan to be saved from total destruction.

"I say, we who watched from our posts of observation in space, lost all hope of ever seeing your planet rescued from the fate it had brought upon itself. And so our interest waned. Except for an occasional visit of compassionate scrutiny, we consigned your planet to oblivion as far as we, personally, were concerned.

"Not so your Redeemer! He had made a sacred promise to those who believed and trusted Him implicitly. To them He said He would return in power and great glory, and this dark orb would be illumined in spite of all efforts of the Dark Ones to prevent it from happening.

"We come now in full confidence that this promise is to be kept. We have been summoned to assist in the fulfilling of this promise. Knowing from long experience the manifold joys and satisfactions which will be yours when you are released from all those who hold you captive to their evil wills, we come with an excess of enthusiasm to lend our support to this crusade. Yet we hold ourselves subject at all times to the All-Wise supervision of our Supreme Commander.

"Before discontinuing, I feel impelled to add one word of counsel. Make your own life conform as nearly as possible with the matchless teachings of One Who humbled Himself to contact mortals in a physical manifestation. Any likeness to Him will enable us to recognize your legitimate claim to our special attention and assistance.

"As future friends and co-workers in the service of your coming King of Kings, we salute you and *WE COME AS YOUR DEFENDERS AND DELIVERERS.*

"*WE COME AT THE URGENT REQUEST OF YOUR*

*HEAVENLY FATHER TO RELEASE YOU FROM INSUF-
FERABLE BONDAGE. MY LOVE AND MY BLESSINGS—
Ashtar, Commander of ten million Space Men, now occupying
bases established within range of your planet."*

• • •

*Continuing with the recent research of Carole Hall, her
next question, closely related to the first, was:*

Carole: "Please clarify the connection between the work
of the Spiritual Hierarchy and the part being played by the
Space Brothers in the Divine Plan."

Ashtar: "Thousands of years ago in Atlantis, it was necessary to seal off etherically the higher planes, of what has been
identified on earth as the astral dimension. This event was the
beginning of the work of the Brotherhood of Light on the inner
planes of Tefra. This resulted in the excessively polarized mental and emotional energies operating on your physical plane. It
focused the attention of contemporary religious teachings on
the 'distance' between the individual and God.

"The crisis which precipitated the withdrawal of the
Greater Light of the astral dimension behind the 'veil,' and the
decision to reopen the two-way communication between the
higher dimensions and the physical plane frequencies during
the Piscean cycle, was the reason for the coming of the Radiant
One into an earth body.

"Before 'breaking the seal,' two-way communication was
virtually impossible because of the accumulated density of negativity which enveloped the planet at the astral level. (As a matter of interest, that astral density has now precipitated to your
physical dimension in the form you recognize as smog. The
burning of ancient hydrocarbons, the very atoms of which contain within their crystalline structure the 'memory' of the
earth's past, join with the continued projection of collective
astral negativity of humanity in a combination which reflects
as what you call 'smog.' If you will note geographically, where

the greatest concentrations of hydrocarbon deposits presently exist on Tefra, it will help you to understand what I am attempting to convey).

"During the time which elapsed between the withdrawal of the Brotherhood of Light in Atlantis and the Piscean Age (while the seal was still in place) our ships acted not only as the *go-betweens,* but as the *communications system.* The guidance which the prophets of old received was relayed from the Spiritual Kingdom to earth, to the particular Initiates who had volunteered to lead their people out of the long-imposed darkness. They were under our surveillance at all times. If your scriptures are read carefully, it will be seen that many such descriptions are given.

"As a result of the advanced technology which we had by then acquired, a direct consequence of our spiritual development, we were given the opportunity to act as the messenger, to penetrate the physical dimension in our craft. It was not that the Brotherhood of Light was unable to penetrate this density which enveloped your planet, but rather that *humanity's ability to receive the Light,* or Truth, was at a bare minimum because of the density of vibrations.

"Thus, we, whom you know as Space Brothers, were given the opportunity to serve in the Light then, even as we do now. This would not be the case if we had chosen not to abide by Cosmic Law. We serve in the vibration of Love, often at great personal sacrifice to the greater whole, in allegiance to the Radiant One. Our message and guiding principle is Peace. We wish to assist in the bringing of Terra into the Intergalactic Federation of Peace and Brotherhood. It is difficult for us to understand why so much resistance is offered to all assistance; why it is that earth beings prefer to give allegiance to the darkness and their illusions rather than to the Light and Truth.

"For many thousands of years, the multitudes of those who serve in the Light have been patiently working to accomplish the manifestation of Oneness. The cycles of 'time' which have been allotted to Terra's evolution are rapidly condensing into one single point where past, present, and future will meld into one. A new and much greater macro-cycle is about to begin. The curtain is soon to be drawn as has been done several times in the so-called 'past' history of Terra. A new beginning is to be made in which the Children of the Light will make rapid strides in consciousness unencumbered by the gross manifestations of darkness. Once again, the veil will be drawn, sealing the door where evil dwells. The opportunity is being given to enter the Realm of Light, and it is hoped that many will avail themselves of this great opportunity.

"Much valuable time will be saved *if you are already attuned to us.* We salute you, O Children of the Light. You are not alone. We shall employ every means at our disposal to bring this planetary crisis to a swift and successful conclusion. Remain alert and maintain your focus in Love, for it is your 'boarding pass' to safety.

"The river runs dark and deep, and the currents are treacherous. Keep thine eye single, and focus it on reaching the other shore. So it will be."

—Ashtar

• • •

A few days later Carole was greeted by Commander Korton:

"My function within the Ashtar Command is communications coordinator. Please remain focused for one moment and we will complete a group connection which you know as a 'conference call' in your communications system."

Then, speaking as one voice in a joint statement, Jesus, Ashtar, Hilarion, Korton, and Aljanon, the statement began:

"In our Father's House there are many mansions. In other words, there exist systems within systems within systems; yet all of these exist within the One.

"This is not an easy concept to comprehend when you

remember that it is only 300 years of earth time since you began to recognize that your geocentric attitudes were invalid, that the higher truth was a greater heliocentric system. Unfortunately, the geocentric pattern still remains fixed in the mass consciousness, making it difficult for most to perceive that any regional, national, or planetary destruction affects the greater whole of which Earth is only a part. This is a holdover from the involution of ego-consciousness whose time is past.

"In truth, planet Earth is a member not only of its solar system, but also of a greater galactic union. It was *to comprehend this greater reality* that knowledge was released to those who could hear and understand in your earth plane *which led to the Space Age.* It was vital to the evolution of the greater scheme of the solar system's evolution and beyond, that Eartheans begin to look upward and beyond themselves to a *greater awareness level.* However, one of the problems encountered has been the serious lack of spiritual awareness on earth. To acquire the secrets of the atom and the God-power locked therein without the *counterbalancing awareness of Cosmic Law is to court disaster.* As has been pointed out repeatedly, the results of such situations in the past have been disastrous, and your planet suffers yet some of the effects. We assure you *THIS WILL NOT BE ALLOWED TO HAPPEN AGAIN,* and it has been to this end that repeated efforts have been made from many dimensions and other worlds, so to speak, to help the leaders on earth to change the direction of their destructive orientations. The efforts on earth's behalf have been met with fear, resentment, and in some cases, destructive retaliation. Be not deceived by the calls for peace voiced by those who dedicate their energies to the perfection of the weapons of destruction.

"Many still see their bodies and physical needs as the center of their worlds. It is the purpose of the Spiritual Hierarchy of each system to guide the evolution of that particular system for which they are responsible beyond this state of limited awareness to higher Truth. It has been only the past 100 years since the public re-introduction of some of the Wisdom teachings which have reawakened many to the existence of the Hierarchy of Masters in your planetary system. As a result of the residual geocentric attitude, the tendency is for Eartheans to think that the Masters assigned to Earth are the only ones who exist. When humanity can begin to think in terms of being a member of the solar system or galaxy, it will be better able to comprehend that all systems are assigned Masters in accordance with the particular levels of evolution; furthermore, all systems, being a part of an ever greater whole, mandates the inclusiveness of all relative hierarchies into levels beyond the ability of the third dimensional mind to comprehend.

"Because they have all evolved far beyond the state of (self) ego-consciousness so prevalent yet on earth, the members of the Space Command (many of whom are *Masters within their own systems*) have answered the call for assistance to Earth. It must be remembered that beyond the personal self lies a level of humanitarian *group-consciousness* attuned to the vibration of Universal Unconditional Love. Here, there is *no greater and no lesser,* for the illusion of duality and separateness has been overcome.

"It is the tendency *during a particular phase of development* to try to make lesser gods of those who represent a more advanced state of existence. This is again the illusion of those who have not yet recognized their *own existence as an expression of Divinity.* It is this lack of spiritual awareness which must be overcome in order to enter into true understanding— *the overcoming of personal unworthiness,* when in fact all are individualized facets of the Divine Crystal, or God-Mind, and each is in varying steps of progress toward the pure expression of that God-ness in a unique way. All are acceptable in the Light of the One.

"Perhaps now it is easier to understand why, at other dimensions of existence, there is no hesitation when the call comes for assistance. All will respond according to their own abilities, skills, and missions.

"Many souls presently in embodiment on earth do not yet recognize the sacred aspect of the coming events on your planet. While it is true that the planet must endure the sufferings of the outpicturings of collective karmic residue of those lifestreams which have inhabited her aura since her manifestation, it is equally true that this purging of gross negativity will have a profound effect on raising of the planetary vibrations to a level which will invite the manifestation of the spiritual.

"This will be an event of great joy—the introduction of the *sixth sacred planet* within your solar system. Those who are dedicated to serving the Light *long ago* made the decision to serve in this great transition. Many who have answered the call have arrived—from other dimensions to assist where they are needed—from other planets, other solar systems, and other galaxies. Some have experienced several lifetimes on earth in order to be able to better identify with the difference in vibrations."

Carole: "But what of the 'space ships'? are such technological means being implemented to assist with the Hierarchy's work in The Plan for planet Earth? *Many ask* why the Masters cannot accomplish what is necessary."

"We see the problem as having several parts. First, we remind you to return to the statement about *making lesser gods of the Masters*. Secondly, there are enormous complex problems involved in this approaching transition. Everything is required to operate under Cosmic Law. The law most applicable here is the *Conservation of Energy*. The organization of the *Greater Plan* requires that all assist in an *interlocking network* according to particular training and skills, with each responsible for a particular aspect of the whole plan. This we have attempted to convey as well to those who serve at this time on the earth plane.

"One of the greatest problems confronting us has been the

development of the program for the preservation of the 'vehicles of consciousness' necessary for continuation in the raised vibration of the earth plane. When evacuation becomes necessary, *it would be impossible to raise the vibration of those on the earth plane sufficiently to override the effects of 'the cleansing' without separating them from their physical vehicles.* Therefore, it is necessary—as it has been other times in the past—to bring aboard the space ships those who have achieved sufficient degrees of purification to be able to tolerate the vibration of the higher force-field. Here the bioelectromagnetics of these problems can be overcome by the advanced technological abilities of the Space Brothers.

"When the earth has been re-stabilized in its new vibration, many of those who have been 'lifted' will return to inhabit the earth in bodies to which their *'vehicles of consciousness'* have been properly attuned. In a way, it could be said that a space ship is quite similar to a physical embodiment, for it is also the vehicle in which one navigates about in time and space.

"It is hoped that many, many souls will soon complete their attunement in physical consciousness so that they may become consciously aware of these approaching events. The overcoming of fear which we assure you, *will act like an anchor* when the time for 'lift-off' comes—in the twinkling of an eye—is of vital importance. There is now occurring through the media in your plane, a barrage of fear and doubt-inducing tools. This is a test of discernment for each soul—the dividing of the way. Remain alert, and listen with your Being! Know that when you attune to the God within, that you will *not be deceived.* The time of decision is NOW! Your faith is soon to be rewarded with increased knowledge. The worlds which lie now within your grasp will be filled with new wonders and increased happiness.

"We join forces at this time to welcome earth's humanity into that new world. The choice is yours. Listen to your heart and know that the Light will prevail over darkness and ignorance of humanity's spiritual birthright.

"We release at this time a blessing—a flood of Light and Joy to all who read and hear these words. YOU ARE NOT ALONE, O CHILDREN OF THE LIGHT. Look into the skies from whence cometh the saving Grace, for ye are truly One in the Light. So Be It." (Conference Transmission from Korton, Hilarion, Jesus, Ashtar, Aljanon).

The Ashtar Command's War Against Evil

Perhaps one of the lesser known missions of the Ashtar Command is its constant surveillance and control of insidious and malicious influences. These have detrimentally surrounded and interpenetrated the planet, producing the cause for spiritual warfare. Speaking of all such influences, Commander Korton, Command Communications Officer, has given us this interesting passage:

"There are those who do come who are not from this allegiance and who have no part in it. They come as observers and for their own ends. They are often highly scientific geniuses and their material to their contacts can be highly impressive— indeed, almost always is. But they have come for the purpose of collecting data for their personal ends and not to give of themselves for the good of the planet. When there is a desire to help the planet, those outside of the Brotherhood are more interested in raising the scientific level of advancement and care not for the spiritual vibrational frequency aspect. Again, their information passed to their own contactees is of highly intellectual nature and impressive to those who receive it. There is no evidence of loyalty or appreciation to those who have jointly labored for the good of this planet for aeons past. These are not of what you would call the 'dark forces,' which is *another allegiance,* but are simply a neutral force when it comes to assistance to earthman in higher principles and laws contributing to his soul growth. There are many worlds out there, Tuella; many galaxies with individual solar systems and within other universes. You have been, and most like you, are in contact with the sources from which you come, within this Universe of Space. But others do also roam the heavens who have full access to all pathways and planets, though they be not of the Commands which guard this planet—especially against itself.

"When Maldek overloaded its technological circuit, so to speak, its sources of technical contact were from beyond this universe. It would not listen nor abide within the framework of bylines of Peace held by this galaxy, but chose to listen to others, and therefore created its own fate. Politics in heaven, you say? To a certain extent, yes, before our consolidation and before the forming of the Great Brotherhood of Light. The Brotherhood of Light is concerned with enlightening the individuals of all of its solar systems in the knowledge of the Creator and His principles of Light and Life. As our Beloved Master has put it in your scriptures, 'For what prosper a man if he gain the whole world but lose (confuse) his own soul?'

"Now the so-called 'Dark Forces' (a balancing agent in the Cosmos) are those of our own galaxy who are openly opposed to the Brotherhood of Light, its principles and standards and goals for mankind and the planet Earth. They would seize the planet if that were possible, to control it for their own purposes, which would destroy the freedom of man. Commander Ashtar has been one of the most staunch defenders of the freedom of mankind and his inherent right to choose, to decide to fashion his own embodiment, without outside pressures put upon him."

• • •

Although I had been told to expect Master Hermes to speak sometime during this book, I was nevertheless surprised when he suddenly did so on September 18, to sound this warning:

"The bands of renegades that patrol the terrestrial realms are immediately dispatched to their proper level when overtaken in trespassing activities. The fleets of the heavenly commands are prompt to transport such intruders in masterly fashion. However, it is on your octave that the enemy must be met and dealt with from a physical vehicle.

"You of the Light, now in physical form, are the ones who must stand in the gap and speak to displace the dark ones who continually strive to interlope their will upon man and intervene in all of his good intentions. The powers of the celestial forces will back you up in these matters, but it is the embodied ones who must challenge the darkness with the Light, on YOUR level. You must learn the power of your weapon of Light, your weapon of invocation, your weapon of declaring your identity with the Christ Forces on all dimensions. You may invoke the presence of the Host of Lord Michael, but having done so, then it is the child of Light who must discern, dispose and disperse the presence of darkness in its midst. For this is YOUR battleground, this is YOUR arena of challenge, and this is WHERE YOUR VICTORY must be won.

"For this cause, as you have been told, many of Ashtar's personnel do now walk your streets and abide with you, where they, in their cloak of flesh, may also enter spiritual combat with the enemy of mankind. I, Hermes, do vouchsafe to you that these extraterrestrial souls do now in the thousands infiltrate every walk of life and service upon your planet.

"These might be termed 'God's Infantry, God's foot soldiers,' if you will pardon the term. So hesitate not to take your stand against evil on inner levels of challenge, and forthrightly, with Michael overshadowing, hold the Light of God over every intrusion of the fallen ones. You are God's Army warring with spiritual weapons in this Battle of the last Armageddon. Ashtar counts on every one of you to join him in the fray of this battle for the Light."

• • •

The following material was shared with us by a former highly active member of the Solar Cross Foundation in California. The passage is taken from their teaching material of that time. (MAN refers to the Space Intelligences).

"The Satonians resemble *MAN* in appearance. The similarity ends there. Their thoughts are negative to the extreme and this negative radiation of thought is the means by which they are detected.

"Positive *MAN* is superior in every way to negative Satonians. *MAN* always is the victor in any confrontation—by the use of The Light. However, the Satonians and their presence *is masked in a negative environment*. The earth has a negative environment at present. The Satonians are driven away, expelled and flee from the Light, when it is directed at them by *MAN*.

"Satonians also have spacecraft. They travel in space the same as *MAN*. However, *MAN* has established reserved areas of space for their use."

Identifying a Spaceship of *MAN* Versus That of a Satonian

"Positive *MAN* will always identify himself and broadcast thoughts of Light and goodwill. You will know, deep within yourself, that this is *MAN*.

"A Satonian will not identify himself in a satisfactory manner and his negative thought force that is radiated is easy to detect. He will flee if one directs the Light at him.

"Never approach a spaceship until you are sure that is it *MAN'S*. And always use the Light in your greeting and approach. *MAN* will welcome it. A Satonian will remove himself from a greeting in The Light ."

MAN'S Functioning

"*MAN* searches the Cosmos for Life and the beginnings of

life. When it is found or conditions are such that life can be a benefit, the Light is used to enhance life itself.

"All life everywhere welcomes the presence of *MAN* and cooperates with *MAN,* for they sense the Light that MAN is. An exception to this is Earthmen's reaction to this thus far, and of course, the Satonians."

• • •

Several years ago I released a series of articles covering my first telepathic encounter with Captain Avalon. In the material a brief discourse was concerned with the negative forces of Space:

"Please discuss the Alien UFO Forces (Dark Forces)."

"There are dark forces. There are those who are evil in their intent. We have had close surveillance of them in the past. Most of them have now been removed through the Guardian Action; a few still remain in Earth's atmosphere. This has been the nature of our work likewise in this area. We are heaven's policemen. We are the watchmen on the walls. We are the Guardian Action. We guard and protect, even as your patrol cars patrol your city streets in the darkness. This we do, constantly on the alert for any ships of the dark forces."

"Captain, what is the insignia on the ships of the dark forces?"

"There are several, but the most active are the Deros from inner space. Their insignias are always painted in black, whatever they might be. Certain forces of six planets of Orion, that have conducted themselves against the Injunctions of the Interplanetary Council, are cordoned off, and are well under control. We have been working on this situation for centuries, but we do now have them under control and they do not reckon in the problems that are in Earth's future. It was very important for the earth that removal was completed before other occurrences begin."

• • •

I choose to share with you some wise words from Jacques Drabier:

Is There Evil?

"Many people seem to be convinced that there is no such thing as evil. It seems this reasoning goes along with the idea that God is dead and that Satan is a myth.

"Anything which deliberately hurts and hinders another individual is evil, and when it is willfully and maliciously designed to do so, it is even MORE evil. The Federation surrounds and defends the earth as much as possible, from the invading ships of individual gods. But it cannot control the minds of the individuals who are easily led to believe that all spacecraft occupants are godlike and good. There are *good and evil,* and the trick is *to know the difference* and to form association only with those who desire and are capable of making life on earth *better* through their own positive understanding."

• • •

In her book INNER VIEWS FROM THE GALACTIC COMMAND, Bonnie Ireland records a message from Captain Tonanias of that Command, which gives further insight concerning the Dark Forces:

"There are those in the Universe who are not as friendly as we. They do not belong to the Universal Brotherhood and only want to destroy and rule. They are small in number, but when they put forth an effort, their strength can be mighty.

"We have been able, by the Hierarchy and the Great White Brotherhood, to act as intermediaries in your defense. It has been a rather strange situation, as we have sometimes been regarded as your enemies and not your protectors.

"How, then, would you know us? distinguish us from your enemies?

"*Always in the Higher forces, the main forms are spheres*

or circles. If a ship is not a sphere, either *elongated,* or a *conical shape* or has some protruding facets attached to it, this can be of a devious nature.

"Please note: We say, *can be.* There are some ships from very distant universes which are of a different shape other than a true sphere, but who have come here in your defense. So here again, you must use another method of determining who is friend or foe. *That method is through vibrations.*

"In this respect it is most important that those who understand start to concentrate on their feelings through vibrations which come from the atmosphere. Learn to understand these feelings and abide by them. The negative forces naturally let off dark, *negative rays which can be felt as a heavy, depressing feeling by the human form, which also creates a feeling of fear or impending doom.* If this happens, please learn to back off from this force as quickly as possible and ask for help. Here again, we use a form of mental telepathy. If you can learn to use the mind-to-mind method now, it will come in great stead for you later on, and might even save your life. Here we might say that if you have already created a channel with us, there will be no problem with communication in the future.

"If and when you call on us for help, we will communicate with you immediately and put a force field of protection around you until such time as your adversary is quelled and forced to disappear until we can transport you out of their reach into another area."

An Interview With Ashtar

Upon hearing the subject of this forthcoming book, a friend thoughtfully forwarded to us the works of Trevor James with which we were unfamiliar. This work, referred to earlier in this volume, contained an informative question and answer session with ASHTAR concerning the Dark Forces' activities. We are deeply indebted to Mr. James for his kind permission to print any of his material we chose to select. The important discourse follows:

Question: "A question that has greatly disturbed me, concerns the presence of an underground race on this planet. I would appreciate any information you can give me." I was hardly prepared for the import and impact of the answer I received. In one stroke it minted a key to the UFO mystery, and dispelled much confusion.

Ashtar: "At the *core* of your planet there dwells a greatly degenerated race, an astral race, which is degenerate not so much in science, but in every moral respect as you know and understand it. They are capable of space flight within the astral regions around the earth, but are earthbound. They are the forces of Eranus, whom you call Satan. They emerge at the South Pole. On your surface, they have allies who are without morals and without mercy. I give you this information that you may be aware of their existence. I enjoin you to forever close any researches into this astral activity, in the interests of your own safety.

"Be on your guard always, be careful and vigilant."

94

A careful review of the communication makes the puzzle more like a picture. First, he speaks of the core of the planet. It is important that we remember that he is speaking of the core, and not of any *intervening* levels of life that may or may not exist. We shall return to this shortly.

Secondly, an astral race is mentioned. This would be a race of finer, differently vibrating beings than ourselves, invisible to us except at certain times and under certain conditions. Degenerate not in science, no, for do they not whisk through our atmosphere in craft of high performance? This was beginning to make sense! The forces of Eranus? Who's he? The being we call Satan! Is there in fact such a being or deity? Could it be that the Bible is not after all the pure trash some scientists regard it as being? Could it be that some of the UFO constitute the air force of this dark deity?

Question: "These astrals from the earth's core are, I take, the 'dero' of legend?"

Ashtar: "No. The Dero are no longer confined in the caves of legend and story, but are reincarnated upon your surface. Many of your eminent scientists, driving forward with the perfection of ever more prodigious blast forces, are reincarnated deros, because of their prior lives as cannibals and degenerates."

Question: "How far from the surface of the earth in our measure, do the astral regions extend?"

Ashtar: "125,000 miles. Within them, the astral beings are confined. At certain times of the year travel to the moon is possible to the astrals when the astral shells of the two bodies overlap. When these two shells separate, however, any entities on the moon are cut off from the earth until the next time the astral shells overlap. *No physical or astral entity* can get beyond the earth-moon system."

Question: "Three-dimensional craft have been seen in addition to the others described in these contacts. They are believed to be of a mechanical type. Are there such ships, and where do they come from?"

Ashtar: "Yes, there are such ships. They come from the continent that you call 'Antarctica'."

Question: "What is the nature of the astral regions around the earth?"

Ashtar: "The astral world is divided into two broad sections. First there are the bodiless entities from our surface, the so-called dead people, who must become incarnate again in order to pass completely to the etheric state. Some of these entities are waiting what will be their last incarnation. Others are those who have had their carnate existence terminated abruptly or accidentally, such as criminals and soldiers. All these entities have in common the intense desire to become fleshly once more, in order that they may qualify to be no longer earthbound when their incarnations terminate. This is the Garden of Waiting. There are also the monstrosities and phantasmagoria which are degenerate thought forms. The other great section of the astral world is the astral regions of evil which surround and interpenetrate the earth, inhabited by beings who are forever discarnate and forever earthbound by decree of the Great God of the Universe. These beings cannot enter the Garden of Waiting. It is against these forces that we of the etheric world are warring."

Question: "What form does this war take? Is it a clashing of space ships in combat?" (Note the childish nature of this question of mine, and marvel at the patience of a highly developed intelligence to whom it was directed).

Ashtar: "It is not a matching of violences, as you suggest, but a *battle for the control of earthly minds.* Our purpose is to overcome the destructive influence, the physically violent influence which the dark ones seek to exert over mankind. Our purpose is to nullify the astral influence by restraining beings devoted to destruction and physical violence. The dark ones seek to relegate the whole world to the darkness wherein they dwell and have power, and thereby increase their influence further. Our task, as decreed by the Heavenly Father, is to nullify, overpower and banish the work of the dark ones by *good influences upon humanity.* This is the true nature of the battle, rather than spacecraft versus spacecraft."

Question: "What is the nature of the core of our planet? Is it solid? Or hollow?"

Ashtar: "The center of the earth consists of matter of a density comparable to air, although it is not air. You would term it hollow in your expression. It is here that the forces of Satan dwell. Near the South Pole they emerge in their craft and circle the planet. Clumsy and primitive by our technology, their craft are still greatly advanced over yours, and they are easily able to outperform and to outmaneuver mechanical aircraft of physical manufacture. They are also considerably faster, being capable of speeds in excess of three thousand miles per hour."

Question: "How far above our surface may (the dark forces) penetrate, and can physical man penetrate this far? That is, will man ever be able, in physical form, to penetrate this far?"

Ashtar: "The limit of their altitude attainment is 125,000 miles. Physical man is also limited to this extension. In the upper portions of it, however, man in the physical form will exist only with extreme difficulty and after years of training and development. As previously described, when the moon's astral envelope or aura overlaps with that of the earth, commerce is possible. At times of contact, the astral entities from the core of Shan travel to the moon."

Question: "What is the nature of life on the moon? Are the moon people physical or astral?"

Ashtar: "The moon people are physical in form and astral in allegiance. They are allied with Satan."

I now wondered if there was any connection between the *craft from "downstairs" and the machines which flew in Atlantis, according to legend,*

Question: "Are these craft comparable to Atlantean machines?"

Ashtar: "They are almost identical with those craft. They are, of course, made of a material that is akin to, but of a higher vibratory form than your own matter. They are, therefore, not normally visible to your optics."

The operative phrase here would seem to be "not normally," and this would seem to check out with the appearing and disappearing UFO which have baffled investigators for so long. Not normally visible but sometimes visible, hence many of the observed UFO which disappear before the eyes.

Logically enough, the next question that arose was how to tell one from the other. Who was who and how can one tell? Can the separate manifestations be identified? I asked once more.

Question: "Is there any broad general method by which the etheric or friendly craft can be distinguished from the astral machines from the center of the earth?"

Ashtar: "As a general rule, you may conclude that all cigar-shaped craft are potentially hostile to your people. These are the craft from the center of the earth which have carried out and are carrying out hostile acts. Our craft are, for the most part, heel-shaped, or disc-shaped. This is a *rule of thumb,* as you term it, for distinguishing between them."

This information could be applied to many sightings, and perhaps some interesting and enlightening conclusions drawn. Ashtar here does not say, mark you, that *ALL* cigar-shaped craft are entirely and invariably hostile. He says "you may conclude." These are general rules, rules of thumb, and *not iron-clad formulae.*

The cigar-shaped craft have been observed starting fires and in other questionable acts, as described by Mr. Harold T. Wilkins in his two books.

Sightings involving clear *shapes* are seemingly in the minority while light manifestations are very abundant. Perhaps there might be a rule of thumb regarding light manifestations.

Question: "Are there any basic rules, even if they are

broad rules, by which the various craft can be identified when they appear solely as light manifestations?"

Ashtar: "There is a broad general rule which may apply for the purpose of identification. It is *not* exact, but is a 'rule of thumb,' as you call it. The true interplanetary craft, the ventlas of our forces will appear to your optics with a manifestation of colored lights, usually green, red, and white. They will sometimes appear constantly red and green, other times they will appear to be flashing. Those of the satanic forces *seldom exhibit color,* but come with white or bluish white manifestations. This should aid you in selecting the ships with which you might have contact."

The ability of people to *misinterpret* these last two messages is *unlimited*. We are given a rule of thumb. And yet, people will persist in interpreting this as, "you said *all* blue lights are *bad*." Things are just not that simple!

The proper course of action is to test the criteria, then accept them or discard them in accordance with what one learns from their use.

Referring specifically in this case to the machines purported to come from the center of the earth, I addressed the following question to Ashtar:

Question: "By whom are these craft manned?"

Ashtar: "They have a variety of beings in these craft. They may be human type entities in the astral body, in every way similar to yourself. They may be elementals, sub-human slaves of the astrals. The silver spheres frequently reported, especially those associated with reports of little men as occupants, are a type of craft launched from the carriers of the dark ones. There are several facts which govern the sightings of these things. In the first place, a combination of atmospheric conditions and the physical condition of the viewer may render them visible. In the case of the monstrosities seen by only one person, this may be the case. Certain physical conditions in the viewer may render them visible to one man when they will not be seen by another man beside him. Hence the common term 'hallucination.' But the man who sees these monstrosities is seeing something very real, and while it can be said that the experience is a subjective one in a sense, it is also a view into the unseen worlds which surround and interpenetrate your own. Great confusion is caused upon your surface by the starving descriptions of little green men, little men in various types of clothing and so forth. Believe me, it would take many books to fully describe the many types of elementals who dwell in the invisible realms."

Question: "On occasions, elementals have been seen stealing water, or water has disappeared in large amounts following saucer sightings. Why is this?"

Ashtar: "Water is a valued commodity in the center of the earth where they dwell. One of the reasons they come to your surface is to steal water, which they do from lakes, rivers, reservoirs and tanks as convenience dictates."

Question: "What can you tell me about ShanChea? How long has it been orbiting the earth? What is its size relative to Schare, the other base you have near us?"

Ashtar: "ShanChea is the earth-child satellite, and has been orbiting your earth now for almost two thousand years since the appearance of Jesus the Master upon your surface. Fifteen hundred miles square, it is a complex assemblage of instrumentation which permits constant surveillance of your surface and the beings upon it. Before very many months have passed, although we will at this time give you no earthly measure of when, ShanChea will pass through the atmosphere of Shan, and a great commotion will be caused by its appearance. It will be visible to physical eyes at that time. Our present altitude is five hundred miles and varies considerably from time to time. Schare is different to ShanChea in that it is a Quadra Station. It is not square, but what you call spheroid. Its purposes are also different in our system."

Question: "What are the present intentions of the dark

ones concerning assaults on our surface?"

Ashtar: "During the next few weeks and months, the astral forces will increase their activities along the western coasts of America. Many of their craft will be sighted. Should aircraft of yours be sent against them, they will be destroyed by the agency of a heat ray. Fires of mysterious origin will occur in the Americas and Western Europe. Explosions and unforecasted weather phenomena are part of their system of attack. Communications will be interrupted and airplanes forced down. Failures in electronic equipment are easily induced by them." (7/17/56).

Question: "Is this heat ray the one which has been reported in some attacks on earth aircraft?"

Ashtar: "Yes. It is a heat ray which has been used to interfere with ignition systems and to start extensive fires in various parts of the world."

The reader must be puzzled as I was as to why the attacks are carried out, and also how, if these weird entities are of a different order of matter to our own, they could interfere with our matter. Also, how could they escape detection? Once more, I asked:

Question: "Many investigators are anxious to know *why* the dark forces cause these crashes of planes and collisions involving loss of life. It is not readily apparent to us, nor exactly how it is done."

There was a considerable pause before the answer, as though this being were wondering whether or not he would tax our credulity too far. The answer, when it came, was jarring, almost shocking, but once again it fitted the facts.

Ashtar: "First let me say that the dark ones are highly desirous of causing destruction to airplanes and do so frequently. They would, if it were possible, bring down many more of them if this action would not result in their being detected by some of your people. The reason for this airplane crashing is really very simple for one who has grasped the concept of astral and etheric realms beyond the physical. Frequently, the astrals desire some particular person for a special purpose. Perhaps a technician, an engineer, or one of special skill or talent. They wish to abduct him, in other words. After an airplane crash, when the person concerned is released from his physical body after his 'death' his astral form is seized and taken to the nether regions. The crashes are brought about by several agencies. First, instrumentation failure, resulting in collision of one kind or another. Secondly, by production of fire, usually in the vicinity of fuel tanks. Thirdly, complete suspension of the entire electrical system of the airplane. Fourth, the use of the force field of their own craft to induce structural failure."

Question: What allegiances if any exist between the Soviets and the dark ones?"

Ashtar: "The question is a difficult one to answer because it causes us difficulty in separating the Soviet people from their leaders. The particular type of Lemurian incarnates now ruling Russia are in direct allegiance with the dark ones through processes of black magic and other powers. The Russian people as you know them are no different from yourself and others. It is necessary therefore every step of the way *to draw the line between the Soviet people and their leaders.* The allegiance is most definitely there between the leadership and hierarchy of the Communists, and the dark forces against whom we war.

"Therefore, if you use this communication draw a very solid and certain line between the Russians and their leaders."

• • •

The December 1983 edition of *Cosmic News*, published by the Cosmic Light Foundation, and edited by channel "Camhael," contained the following message from St. Germain:

"The time is coming and IS NOW GOING ON for the changes and for the removal of those who are fighting in darkness, in ignorance, and those who are puppets of the evil ones, who are causing the fight—the war, one might say, of Armageddon. It is of the mind and of the soul energies that those of the evil ones want to destroy so that they can make puppets and slaves of humanity. It is crucial now and it is time now for the Light Workers to follow the teachings, the True Teachings, of Jesus, the Christ, and the Father, and to put down the negative forces. For it truly is a war between the Light Servers and those who would usurp the Light for their own evil ways of power.

"There are not as many evil ones as you might think, who are in control of the world at this time, and they are frightened because of the much Light put forth by those who are working in Light. They are taking a last stand trying to infilter the minds of the True Souls of Light, so that they can steal their soul Light and block their minds of the True Peace Beyond Knowing with the false peace they are putting to enslave the people by their mechanization machinery, by bringing irritation in souls of those in Light and the puppets that they have duped who are, you might say, soulless and mindless at this time. The evil ones have taken their energies, their true Light energies and used them against those of Light. They are stirring up factions of petty wars and arguments all over the earth, in organizations, institutions and even in business, economics and causing irritation, causing true and false factions to usurp the true facts with their lies and with their so-called powers which are really the energies of the souls they have in slavery.

"If the souls in Light would convert their energies into the right factions, into the Light Beings that are in Government, that are in business, that are in the countries where the warring is being initiated; if they would step forth and flow their Light in greater energy, put forth their energies to bring the right, the true teachings and justice into effect, those of the darkness would be removed from the earth. The evil ones know this; that is why they are bringing such irritation and only a few truths filled with false lies, even of peace, that they are saying

103

they will bring to the earth, for their own satisfaction. They do this to take the last energy from the souls whom they are duping, and to tap the energies of those of Light who are not standing up for the Light, who are not flowing the Light as they should but who are in, you might say, an ignorant state of lethargy not knowing which way to turn and not flowing the Light. They are the 'pacifists' who are on the fence who, if they stood For the Light and flowed the Light, could bring forth the turn of Glory, Peace beyond knowing, True Eternal Life into their own souls and thus usurp the false powers of the evil ones who are the fallen angels, and nephilim and the fallen watchers.

"This must be done to usurp the negative forces of the evil ones. This must be done through each one's free will, through the Light servers using their Light Powers."

• • •

Oscar Magocsi's FEDERATION contact is ARGUS, Resident Director, earth-assigned, Psychean Mission. He speaks of the dark agents:

"Many a time in the past 3–4 years, we of the friendly space powers knew about the intimidating harassments and psychic attacks by the Dark Forces on our friends, Light workers, UFO researchers, associates and sympathizers. We were often on top of the situations, yet we chose not to interfere (except in cases of grave danger)—but rather draw the dark agents out into the open and let them lead us to their connections. In this fashion, we managed to expose and neutralize vast segments of their operational network.

"We apologize for such utilization of friends as bait, but the cleanup job had to be done. Also, some of you wished to help fight cosmic evil. So all was not in vain. Many of you became much stronger and/or underwent much needed (and unavoidable) purification through these past trials and tribulations. And all this helps the global balance shifting towards the

Light. Unfortunately, evil in its many forms and ways is still with us, in spite of rumors to the contrary. Some might say this notion about evil is just paranoia, but is it really? Take a look at happenings in the world. Do you seriously believe that all the senseless malevolence and violence, all the global or personal 'disasters' are just random or coincidental stuff?

"These are times of trials and tribulations. The end of the era is nigh—the only question is the 'when' and the 'how.' The 'end' (or the new beginning) could come any time between 1984 and 1996, but by 1999 the very latest. *Beyond 1984, our Space Federation will no longer make major efforts to avert global disasters—we will rather, shift the emphasis to immediate mass evacuation of earth's decent folks in concert with other allied Space Powers, to be ready whenever the final hour strikes.*

"The next two years (1983 and 1984) or so will bring *much cosmic acceleration to your world*. This will manifest in *individual lives*, as well as in *global affairs*. There will be many more dramatic happenings and strange encounters, sightings and insights, profound changes, social upheavals and natural calamities. This period will also bring long awaited answers and solutions, relief and upswings for most of our friends and sympathizers."

● ● ●

In the past year or so, a diabolical effort was released and surprisingly made its rounds through several otherwise discerning publications. The article exclusively attacked all Light Workers and took on the task of destroying all faith in what was polarized as "The Fallacy of the Space Brothers Religion." Amused at this ludicrous bigotry, I nevertheless realized that none past the first initiation would be influenced by it whatsoever. However, I asked Commander Ashtar to discuss the concept of a Space Brothers Religion. In characteristic poise, he calmly answered:

105

"Religion is a difficult word to employ. The connotations that surround it make it difficult to clarify its meaning. To speak of a Space Religion implies that one has a choice to make from many. This is, as you have realized, a conception of darkness.

"We do not foster, promote, or in any way propagate religion. There is only one Father, One Truth, one Pathway for any soul. Only the unenlightened would speak of a Space Religion. Religious categories of all kinds—and there are no exceptions —are the fruit of the third dimension. They do not apply beyond it, for beyond it the spiritual unity of all things is fundamental. There are dimensions. There are evolutionary grades of progress. But there is only unity in the oneness of Truth; the integration of the Whole of Creation and the One Source of All That Is.

Universal principles just *ARE,* uncolored by any man-made category. To indulge in such mechanisms of terminology is the evidence of not having lifted up the eyes to the total picture, the greater Understanding of the Divine Program and Purpose for mankind. There is but one Program, one Pathway, one Mission: The expansion of Light upon the planet, the coming of the Kingdom of God on Earth as it is in heaven worlds, the integration of Divine Science into the life patterns of mankind, in their highest capacity for acceptance of Divine Heritage, Man—in the image of God!

"Many influences from other dimensions have labored as one to contribute to the fulfillment of this Plan, through countless ages. Be they Ascended Masters, Hierarchal authorities, high council representatives, men and women of other evolved worlds, organized armies of Light—all are one in the binding unity of the goal to raise the frequency of Terra.

"Therefore, to enter into a debate of any kind to malign or praise any certain segment of the unified assault against ignorance and darkness is self-revealing as to its source. *For there is no competition in the Divine Program.* There is no aggrandizement of one category above another. To therefore misuse the human energies for the purpose of attack upon a certain segment of the unified program of Light is an attack upon the Light itself and clearly reveals its source to any discerning soul.

"Only the soul who is unrealized, or responding from a human emotional level, a 'reed shaken by the wind,' would be drawn into such a debate.

"For as long as there is life and breath, there will be opposition to *cloud the pathway* and to *sharpen the discernment* of weaker souls. Remember what The Beloved once said to His disciple when the opposition of another was emphasized. The Master replied, 'What is that to thee; follow thou Me!'

"Run not to and fro, and to the right and the left to answer thy accusers, but walk thy pathway with a conqueror's tread, and the Beloved, who is thy shield and buckler, shall be thy refuge."

Beloved ones, it is clearly indicated that in this war against evil and the battle for the minds of men, the Guardian Action is a responsibility shared by both those of the Ashtar Command and their earth-based warriors as well. Stand in the Christ Light, and learn to use it. This is our only defense 'against the evil that besets our world. Remember the affirmation:

I AM...a Guardian of the Light!
I AM...Love in Action Here!
cooperating
with the
ASHTAR COMMAND!

● ● ●

In conclusion of this portion of our text, we order this final message from Ashtar, which was recorded by Carole Hall in July, 1984:

"The numerous space vehicles of which you are constantly aware at the present time are but a part of the vast fleet standing at attention and readiness in the vicinity of planet earth.

"Although there have always been manned space vehicles in the etheric dimension, modern man has not been publicly aware of such phenomena until the introduction of mass communication during the past 50 years of the 20th century.

"Prior to that time, many were able to be seen by those who had extended sight, and occasionally, ships would lower their vibration and enter the physical dimension for various purposes which cannot be disclosed at this time.

"The increasing materialism of human consciousness over the past several centuries has greatly clouded man's ability to see and understand these manifestations for what they are.

"It is true that these vehicles and their occupants have come from other planets—some even from other galaxies and solar systems, and though the appearance of some may vary from the form of earth humanity because of varying stages of evolution, you may be assured that they come as 'bearers of the One Light which pervades all Creation.'

"Many attempts have been made by certain energies on earth who are strongly magnetized to the darkness to make it appear that these 'space beings' as you call them on earth, are destructive and should be regarded with fear and distrust.

"It is truly unfortunate that such untruths are so readily absorbed by so many who still remain focused in matter.

"In truth, Planet Earth in your solar system is known as a *dark star*, and it has no attraction, therefore, for more highly evolved beings because it is still so strongly focused in the illusion of matter. Just as earth beings are still very much attached to earth and its immediate surrounding atmosphere, so, too, are all other beings of such relatively unevolved consciousness on other planets such as earth. For the universal knowledge of interplanetary space flight is by cosmic law *not allowed to be released* into the mental plane of a manifested planet until such time as the *mass consciousness has evolved out of the state of matter consciousness;* in other words, has achieved the opening of the Heart Chakra or higher. Thus focused in the spiritual dimensions, the energies are incapable of being used negatively in any destructive way.

"Those 'space' beings who have entered earth's system have come to serve the humanity of earth, not to harm. They have achieved such levels of self discipline and awareness of cosmic law, which disallows death and destruction of any life form, that they are incapable of causing harm.

"This concept, we know, is a difficult one for the three-dimensional mind which has not yet detached from the fears locked into the subconscious; however, it is a state which will be overcome in the Aquarian Age, for it acts like an anchor inhibiting the evolution of consciousness.

"The beings who enter Earth's environment have achieved both fourth and fifth dimensional consciousness, and have come to help teach humanity on Earth how to use the mind to create consciously all that he needs. This information will not be given, however, until after the earth's purification so that it will not be used to control or manipulate others or to destroy. First, all such destructive negative patterns must be erased from the subconscious. Mankind is presently incapable of imagining the many wonders which await him in the not-too-distant future. Much cosmic truth will be revealed in the future which will greatly alter and speed the progress on earth.

"It is important that earth beings learn to understand that they have nothing to fear from the space beings. Rather, they have much to learn from them."

—I am Ashtar

III
Ashtar and The Message

Messages Applicable Individually

In our reprinting of the messages of Ashtar that have gone before, we can appreciate the continuity of his message, the burden of his heart for humanity, that has basically never changed regardless of the identity of his messenger. His concern for the freedom of mankind, his Universal statesmanship and intergalactic diplomacy in the cause of Universal Peace flows through every contact.

We present these remaining messages arranged as:

A. Messages applicable individually.
B. Messages for the World Servers and Light Workers.
C. Messages to whosoever will consider his words.
D. Messages of Worldwide and Global significance.
E. Messages to World Leaders and World Conspirators.

The first is an unpublished message received a few years ago.

The Greatest Freedom of All

"In the beginning of the contact of the brothers from other worlds, there was great despair. Conditions upon the planet left little cause for rejoicing. Souls had lowered their vibrations so far beneath the original plan ordained for them by the Great Lord, that their activities brought only sorrow to those who came to help.

"With the passing of time and cycles, there was a continual infiltration of the men and women from other worlds who came into the fleshly form and walked the earth for the purpose of lifting its vibrations. This action of the Divine Plan lasted for many thousands and thousands of years, and continued expanding from time to time through many cultures and civilizations.

"As one studies the past history of mankind upon the planet and learns of the individuals who played so prominent a place in that history, one is able to discern the identities of the Light Beings. The advancements they brought, the enlightenment they shared, the inventiveness, the expertise, the inheritance they left upon the planet in every field of human endeavor, speaks plainly of the origin of these great mentors and benefactors of humanity. Thus the upliftment went on.

"There were those who had come to offer their great abilities and wisdom, who were contacted on inner levels by those of other worlds. Often they were not aware of the source of their contact, or its nature or the manner of its transmission or reception. They would accept the messages to be the voice of God and the guidance of God. But even then, so very long ago, there were those who were aware of these things and could look upon those who spoke with them, and behold their countenance and perceive their appearance, and know that One from a Higher Realm spoke with them and stood beside them. Since the dawn of time, there have ever been those souls incarnate who could consciously enter into fellowship and exchange of thought with the Watchers of the planet. World scriptures are filled with these incidents—perhaps the most memorable being that moment in the garden, when the Master Jesus was seen in conversation with two members of the Higher Realms. Thus Light has penetrated, Light has expanded, Light has lifted the world in which you live.

"Nevertheless, there ever remain those who choose the darkness; those who refuse the Light; those who willfully will not enter a better way or present themselves that they might become enlightened and open to the things of Spirit and the things of Outer Space. We may not intrude upon their choices when the human will has so decided. For on the earth, there exists the right of freedom of choice and the exercise of freedom of will. The other worlds do not have this arrangement. It is unnecessary, for all hearts are in harmony with Light and the will of God and the knowledge of God. No policing is necessary, and there is no need of this freedom of will in other worlds, for all choose that which is best. All are so captivated by the Love of God and the Presence of His Spirit, that they automatically do that which is the good and choose that which is the best, and walk in Light.

"Those who have totally surrendered their lives and their will into the hands of the Loving Father, have themselves moved beyond a point where freedom of will is the guidance of their lives. For even though they remain incarnate upon your planet, they have advanced to that spiritual standard wherein their every desire and their every choice, their every decision is in harmony with the mind of God. When a soul has attained this stature, then no longer does the law of freedom, of will apply, when every act, every word and every thought is in harmony with the universe. *There is no freedom that can compare with the freedom to do and to be that which is in harmony with all of Life and all of Divine Mind throughout infinity.*

I have desired to share these thoughts with all. I am Ashtar."

• • •

From the channeling of an earlier contactee, Marian Hartill, in 1968, Ashtar spoke on Love:

"I wish to speak to you this day concerning the act of meditation. We have asked you whom we serve to spend at least one hour a day to send out thoughts of love to help us in balancing the negation we must constantly overcome in our work.

113

"We see among you a great conflict as to how to go about this without the guilt of taking time from 'things that really need doing.'

"The secret of sending out love and light is in remembering what love FEELS like. Sit back and remember being in love; you have those feelings all within you. Go back in time if need be, and pick up those emotions of being so enraptured by another being that you floated on a cloud of pure happiness when you could spend hours upon hours just enjoying the feel of being needed, cherished and adored by that love in your life.

"The sad truth is that most of you have forgotten how to feel love and send it out from yourselves to others. This is an illness of your time, a result of overemphasis on sex as the total end—or that which should satisfy every need.

"How much you miss in not practicing the act of receiving love—not only in what we wish to send you, but from others around you because you feel you must read the paper, turn on the radio or television. *In doing this you dull the sensitive receptive centers of your being to the vibrations of love that are around you.*

"It is you who have dulled your minds and hearts to the vibrations of we who seek desperately to aid you by refining your emotions and teaching you once more to FEEL.

"If we asked a person who was truly in love to meditate, and send out love to that loved one, they would laugh and say, 'He's a song in my heart; I sing it day and night. I'm never alone because I feel his (her) love around me.'

"Go back and remember how it feels to love, and then you will see what it is we need and it will not be a chore, but just a love song sung by hearts that yearn to know truth, freedom, and a oneness with their God-self. I am Ashtar."

• • •

In loving consideration, Ashtar has discussed balance in the life of a disciple:

"The pacing of time in the life of a disciple is important in accomplishing all that must be done for the Light in the shortness of time that remains. Multitudes of voices call and lure the inspired one away from their best avenue of expression. Pleasure and pursuits of a secular nature are ever present to detour the dedicated Light worker from the task. But those who have traveled far along the Pathway have come to recognize all such interference and are not thus distracted.

"However, I do stress the necessity of a time of coming apart to rest awhile, as taught by the Beloved, as very necessary. The great masters of the delicate concert instruments lovingly release the strings of their treasured instruments and allow them a time of loosening the tautness and the tightness and give them a rest, that their instrument will be all the more prepared to serve when the next appointment comes. There must likewise be space in the life of the most ardent devotee for relaxation of the pressures and the pull of great responsibilities. There must be a time of infilling the divine energies. Do not deny yourselves moments of withdrawal into peace, for when you return, the battle will still be there to be fought and won."

I have appreciated those words, and I am also reminded that without the "rests" music would lose much of its beauty!

• • •

This unpublished message on the dominions of heaven was given for the Master Symbol of the Solar Cross book, but was not included in its final form. It is worth repeating here:

Divine Order in Heaven

The levels, or planes of heaven as they are sometimes called—and incorrectly so—in reality refer to the dominions or levels of Hierarchy that are the divine government in any Hierarchal system. A Hierarchical system refers to a galaxy of worlds within the solar systems of that galaxy. There are dominions and principalities and levels of spiritual status within each plateau of authority within each galaxy. The same applies, however higher in the interstellar structure of worlds one rises. There is always Divine Order and divine dimensions thereof.

Greatness is not the distinction, but ascension in spiritual stature, abilities and accomplishments represented by the many initiations.

The location of the central government of each dimension or plane is likewise the location of that central sun, or government. The dimension or rank within the dominions always represents the attainment of those within it.

In your world, those who have attained that right to represent the rest of the people through having come through many initiations, so to speak, to reach that privilege, are all gathered together at your seat of government in your Capitol. Likewise on lesser levels, or state and county levels, lesser dominions preside, yet the lesser is a part of the higher and the higher is a part of the lesser, for all is American government.

The Great Central Sun is the seat or location of the Divine Government, or principalities and dominions of this galaxy, representing there the highest dimension, just as within each separate solar system there is divine order representing dominion or government for that solar system as well as those who represent dominion for a planetary level or body. Just as your earthean countryside is represented as city, county, state, national and international governing bodies, so the Universe is likewise one of order in its dominion. And those dominions are that which, in the past, because of lack of Understanding and Knowledge were referred to as levels or planes of heaven. Each division of order represents high frequencies of attainment (i.e., responsibility—for the greater the attainment, the greater the responsibility). Thus, souls do progress from one planet to another, one solar system to another, one galaxy to another in the progression of attainment. Thus you see the names, as

116

such, of levels and planes is irrelevant, for at each point of location of order on any level of dimension or dominion, there are twelve levels or initiations to be attained, with twelve lessons within each initiation. All persons on one certain planet may not all be striving toward the same attainment. You may be progressing within the steps of the tenth initiation, while your neighbor down the street may be just entering the second lesson of the first initiation. Yet both of you have chosen to enter these initiations on the earth dominion (I speak not now of volunteer assignments, who are basically teachers of the initiates).

This subject is not as complex as at first it appears. All one needs to realize is that there is divine order in all things—*as above, so below.*

• • •

It has continued to be a mystery to me why my devotional contacts have included such a preponderance of persons whose names begin with "A." As strange as it seemed, I was not prepared for the strange explanation I received from Ashtar on the subject:

Question: "Sir, please explain what all of the A's mean in my contacts."

Answer: "'A' is Alpha, the beginning. 'A' is first—the wayshower. 'A' is airborne. 'A' is pointed toward heaven while it stands upon its own two feet. It resolutely points to a high dimension of attainment. Ashtar (Command, Alliance [of planets]), Avalon, Athena, all who have come to you using a first letter 'A' have done so because of the symbolism of the aggregate 'A's' in their symbolism of beginnings. All of the 'A's' you have encountered are souls of the elder race who, in the beginning of time have vowed together in the Brotherhood of Light a certain vow that would bind them to the earth until its glory had come. Athena, Anton, Arunada, Armeda, Amorania—and there will be many more—are code names to you to identify those who have taken this vow with you in ancient days. Of course, there are others with other letters, other names, who have likewise participated, but those coded 'A' have a special togetherness and will always be so. Every old letter is a symbol of sorts, indicating various degrees of mission to the planet in the original covenants. The 'T's' you know as integration, so often one will, in an earthly journey, take upon itself another letter which is tied to the details of that incarnation. Teska, Tuella, Tarvis, Thedra, have their own overtones, just as every other Greek letter has also. Korendor and the Korendians have a very special ministry to this planet that has been expedited many times in ancient days. The letter 'K' gives them their distinction and the nature of their work within the galaxy. So it goes on. But you have been correct in realizing there was more than coincidence in the preponderance of 'A's' in your spiritual contacts. We could have some interesting sessions taking the letters one by one through the traces of association, but time does not allow.

"I am your loyal friend and brother in the Light of our Beloved Commander and His Mission to Earth. I am Ashtar."

• • •

At one time in the past, I had asked Ashtar to discuss the human forcefield, and he replied:

"The magnetics of the human aura are a forcefield. The heart is the central atom around which neutrons, cells and electrons gravitate. Blood goes out from the heart, makes its circle and returns again, enabling the physical form to give off energy in frame work as force. Force continues in an ovoid shape which you call the auric field, but it is more than that. This force represents a magnetism to other magnetic force of like frequency. So like attracts like, it is said. Now, when the field is of high frequency, color disappears into white Light. When the human orbit or magnetic field is white light, we then say that one has transmuted the physical form of density to a Light body. This Light body or forcefield is that which makes contact and exposure to our magnetic field possible. You would suffer no discomfort in our presence. The forcefield of Light pulls and is pulled ever higher. Your constant exposure to our frequencies greatly infuses your own with higher frequencies."

While preparing this text, he said that, "While within our great Mother Ships of my own Command fleet and hosted by our staff, you will be subjected to many different kinds of experiences designed to correlate your physical with your spiritual attainment. The physical form will take on great beauty and an essence of Light will radiate to those with eyes to see. The entire being will become changed into that which you once were, yet when you return those who know you not will simply continue to see that outward appearance. But spiritually aware persons will see the difference in the eyes, the magnetism and the glow of the person, and the radiance of the countenance."

I asked if this change would take place within all who attended?

"Yes, but with some who have not started this process at all, the workings will only have begun, so the immediate change will not be so noticeable as with those in whom the process began some time ago. Those who are just beginning will sense youthful energy so that they feel exhilarated; with others, it will be completed. Minds also will be quickened by the rays in which you will sit, and the emotional body will be brought under total control and instructions and directives given. Youthfulness of action and appearance accompanies the presence of the Light body. Generally speaking, those who know not your inner qualities will see your appearance the same, yet there will be that different quality about you somehow. They will say you're 'looking good,' and that sort of thing. But to those spiritually aware of your Light, you will appear much younger, youthful of energy and movement. The presence of Light itself within the physical form tends to rejuvenate and reactivate all the cells of the body; thus, no illness can enter this teeming life action, and the energy that enters

119

find no impediments to its flow. Therefore, the change into the Light body brings these outward changes as a result of the inner workings of the Light. It is a natural as well as scientific action, actually. In the completion of this action one has desire for a lesser quantity of food and tends toward drinking of more liquids."

• • •

Through his fine channel, Mrs. E.P. Hill, Ashtar promises us:

"Once thou hast contacted these currents of Cosmic Energy penetrating with ever-increasing potency the finer, etheric Life Force all about thee, no heavy, clogging earth vibrations can hold thee in thraldom to disease of body, mind or spirit.

"Until the Day of the Great Illumination, there will unavoidably be a struggle to attain and maintain at all times content and perfect attunement with this Divine Source of Life and Love Triumphant! Yet, herein doth lie thy freedom from the fretting exigencies arising from incessant friction twixt the fast receding customs and systems of a decadent and expiring age and that glorious New Age of unexplored marvels along every line of constructive and progressive effort."

• • •

Through White Star is given this communique by the Ashtar Command, titled "Emotional Stability in A Crisis":

"There are factors concerning our operations in the future that will necessitate a greater awareness on your part of the methods used by our FORCES. Our BEAM sent forth to those who are receptive and have been prepared, can only be effective when the recipient is emotionally stable, and for this reason a program was given to you so that you would consciously work on this factor.

"You will note in all cases of calamity there are those who

PANIC and there are those who advance with precise action. The latter are those who are powered by *FORCES* that rush forth adding great power of direction and fortitude to the one so stabilized as to be a *DIRECT FOCUS* for the God-sent Ambassadors to utilize.

"Remember, in all cases of *SEEMING* miracle, there have appeared what man has *recorded* as 'Supernatural' forces. 'Supernatural' forces do not exist, but only *NATURAL FORCES* that appear so to the limited concept of Earth man. Man of Earth has turned his ear and his senses from the *NATURAL* and has limited his abilities by so doing. Isolating himself from the *SOURCE OF LIFE*, he has developed a consciousness of self that renders him senseless to the *ANGEL FORCE* that overshadows, and consequently defenseless in the face of violent *NATURE FORCES*.

"Man's animal sense leads him into traps that his *ANGEL SENSE* would *cause* him to *avoid*. The objective mind can deduce only by outer observation, which is limited to the senses of sight, sound, smell, and touch. When chaotic conditions exist in the outer, these senses are not dependable, as only turmoil is registered. The instinctive sense responds and flight or rigid panic are the result, while the one who *knows stability* flows with the condition; moves with the surety of Divine Direction.

"The destruction of human forms in the face of Nature's rampages can be greatly curtailed by *STABILITY OF ACTION*. A *whole flock* can be saved by the intelligent action of one shepherd. One shepherd under *Divine Direction* can lead masses to safety. One man so attuned to his Angelic Nature can be a *saviour* to many.

"We can and do work directly through those who are capable of our assistance. We have trained thousands for *Stations of Direct Contact Control*. Meaning that in a moment of emergency they become immediate 'machines' for the Higher Forces. The Ashtar Command."

Messages to World Servers

The following discourse was found. in an old file of a child of Light who long ago translated to higher realms. This transcription was received in 1955 by a group where Elouise Moeller was channeling Ashtar. Elouise was the compiler of the lessons from Venus, called simply, *The Science of Living*, probably out of print now, but they once appeared in the magazine *Chimes*, edited by June Denton. The transcript for the evening follows:

"Since the success of my contacts with our brethren of earth has been brought about in interstellar space, in other solar systems beyond this of which earth is a part, many more have become interested in our mission, and we have a tremendous number of Light Bearers who are willing to give of themselves in their service to our brethren of earth.

"I knew you would be glad to hear this, for it assures the success of the plan which was formulated a number of years ago when we drew near to this troubled planet and heard the calls for help from the hearts of many of your earth brethren.

"They called to God. They called to Allah. They called to their various gods and goddesses in whatever language they would speak their names, and we heard.

"We were called into this service by the FATHER of us all. The great angels which I contact have long had their link with you of earth, but there did not seem to be the change in the direction of human thought that had been hoped for and therefore, when the call became stronger, we, too, were invited in to take part in this, and this is the call which we have long waited.

"We knew it would one day come. We did not know how it would come about, but for many centuries we have watched the earth planet for the appearance of the Lighted Landing Fields such as this consecrated home in which we of outer space are meeting with you of earth. The high light-bearing angels of God are also taking part in this evening's hour.

"They bring a special power. We bring a special power, and you who are endeavoring to live a life of right, are also giving forth a special power. This three-way consecrated power is being used as a great motive power over which at this moment tremendous waves of light-bearing atoms are being propelled through the ethers of the earth and certain devastated regions of the earth which we hope you will remember in prayer at the conclusion of what we have to say tonight. Certain devastated regions are being held especially in the Light.

"When we see that a certain level of receptivity has been reached, we can give a more definite work to you.

"Questions have been asked why there are not more of the space ships seen in the skies. We would like to answer that by saying that they are there. It is not necessary for them to be seen in such great numbers at this time for the work. The learning that was occasioned by the sight of our brethren of earth beholding these shining vessels of love and service to you of earth in the skies has served its purpose, and they are now on other missions. However, the time will come when great fleets of them, vast armadas, will be seen in the skies, and that will tell you who are drawn so close to our hearts that another phase of our work has begun. At that time we expect the conditions to be propitious for the taking of those who are inwardly prepared on shorter or longer journeys. We know you are all longing for this. We hesitate ever to cause disappointment in any heart, and yet we must say that in some cases, the physical body could not take such a flight.

"It must be a body in perfect physical health, in a certain

type of spiritual attunement, in a certain degree of soul evolvement and in a state of mental alertness and readiness. We are doing all in our power to prepare as many of our brethren for this as is possible, but we cannot at this moment say who shall or who shall not be the first to have the privilege. But we can say this to you: as days and weeks and years go on and certain conditions are changed in the atmosphere of the earth which will naturally repercuss on the bodies of our earth brethren and in the emotional bodies and in the minds of our brethren, that naturally much of what may have now precluded you will be overcome and others who could not at this moment be taken would at a later time be ready for the journey.

"I find that by the question and answer method we are able to bring to you much that we might otherwise overlook, so now I open the hour for your questions, my brethren."

Question: "When you spoke of the healing that will take place that will prepare people to go on these space ships, does that mean when the dark forces are overcome, or will there naturally be more harmony in the earth?"

Ashtar: "There will naturally be much more of a harmonious condition on the planet when the testing forces are no longer needed in the measure that they are now on the earth. My particular reference was, however, to the physical ills and ailments that afflict so many: what you call 'heart trouble' or 'hardening of the arteries,' or those conditions which would preclude your being taken on a journey which would cause you excitement. Would not that be a natural thing to feel a little bit afraid about it? And therefore, those conditions would naturally preclude the sufferers, and unfortunately, there are all too many who suffer from these conditions, and many of them are spiritually attuned. One of the great purposes of these groups is to bring healing power. There are great healers linked to us in the solar system and there are great healers linked with you from the spiritual realms—the realms of a different substance from ours—the rather solid planets like your earth upon which we have our mental bodies. They are tangible and that also can know dissolution, as your earth bodies, when we choose to lay them down.

"This healing comes not only into the physical body, but it comes into the emotions of the human mind, for there are divisions that need to be healed. When the complete healing has come into the mind and into the emotional body of our earth brethren, there will be no longer concepts between the races. That is one of the important factors we have come to heal—the sense of division, of separateness from other races and nations and other ideologies that are in the consciousness in all too prevalent a form.

"These schisms—these divisions—are, in part, causing some of the physical ailments that afflict the body and the minds of our brethren. When all is in full and complete brotherhood—in full and complete recognition of the oneness of all—when allegiance is given to the one great source of all, much will then fade into the limbo of forgotten things.

"This is a portion of the healing that we would bring into these groups. As you become healed of these divisions in consciousness and thought, and we know you who are here are willing to be healed, and there must first be that willingness before we can step into that work. For you know that you are creators in God and have complete free will, and we recognize that free will. But when the time has come and you have been completely willing to be lifted into that high consciousness of absolute oneness, which some of you think you have, but very few of you have, in reality, then there will come the time when you will find in your midst your brothers of different colors and different races, and we will be able to do work of a higher texture among you.

"When this amalgamation has taken place in consciousness, and not only in consciousness, you will know when it has preceded fully into your consciousness by the effect. By that time you will see the members of the different races among you in groups like this. They will feel the way is open. They will be drawn to you and there will be those of a spiritual calibre like yourselves.

"When that time comes you will be much more ready to receive us who are also of a different order of beings, and yet completely one with you in consciousness.

"We have proven it by coming to you. When the consciousness has opened to the point when you can come to us, then we can appear to you as we are.

"Is there another question?"

Question: "When this healing force takes place on earth as it should be, will the medical profession accept it?"

Ashtar: "The medical profession will be in the midst of it. They cannot help but accept it. There are many in the medical profession who are calling for help, and as these scientists in medicine accept and utilize this which we bring, others will follow in their tracks, and so, the medical profession is also being lifted in consciousness. There are those in the medical profession who would feel perfectly at home here with us. Try to seek them out. The way will be open for them to come. They will become the pioneers."

Question: "Those who have transcended the earth concept of the Guardians of our planet and who have aspirations to work with and cooperate with them but by chance they are taken away from the earth plane before that is realized—what is their condition in the after-death life?"

Ashtar: "My brother, they come straight to us, if they are fully prepared. There is one whom our channel knows who is known as Marcus, who was taken out of his earth body very suddenly. I stood there to receive his soul. He did not even know he had passed from the earth plane by the impact of the two automobiles. He is working on SCHARE. He has one of my earth stations in his care and he was in complete control of the work being done. He was very close in relationship to the ones who care for my beloved amanuensis in Colville, and he

126

came directly to these realms and is working with me, Ashtar, and with others who compose the combination of my closest co-workers.

"Then there is one whom some of you know as 'C.N.' He left his earth form about twenty years ago. C.N. was working on some means of communication between the realms of spirit and the earth. I became aware of his ideas, which were in uniformity with my own. The contact was made and he was what you would call a discarnate soul. He is working most closely with me in the work which we are doing from Venus. Does that answer the question? Nothing is lost. Not one whit of preparation that you make here to link with us is lost. It is all utilized by the Father who is inspiring you to do that."

Question: "What are we to understand by this atomic force—is it for good or evil?"

Ashtar: "Oh, my brother, it is for great good. We utilize that force in our homes; we open our doors by that force; we light our lights by that force; we use that force in our gardens to turn on whenever there needs to be irrigation to bring forth beautiful flowers and shrubs. We use it in a million ways, for it is a great inner cosmic force which has much power in it. The force which is of danger is the *hydrogen force*. The atomic force is of an inert nature. The hydrogen force is a living force and no man on earth can say where that would end in destruction.

"For that reason we have used every power at our command to reach through to the hearts and minds of all those who are in control of these forces of destruction, and we are succeeding. I think you all know why he asked that question."

Question: "There is one man who claims he has been on a space ship and has written a book regarding same, who has a completely different method than the other persons who have claimed this. Is there such a person who is working with the dark forces?"

Ashtar: "As we come to the earth planet, we come to bless and not to destroy. When we come, the testing forces are also released. When our channel asked us the same question you now asked, we said this to her, and we will say no more, for you must learn by your own innermost intelligence that tells you the truth—which is the truth and which may be the truth in another form. I said to this channel, Venus is a large planet. There may be a section of the planet on which such things exist as the young man speaks of, for there are many countries on Venus as there are countries on earth, and things exist on one part of your earth planet that do not exist on another part. I leave the subject for your meditation."

Question: "The question has been asked among our group a number of times about Venusians' method of obtaining their needs. In one of the books the author speaks of the space ships being supplied with enough food for three months. The question is, are these provisions obtained through alchemy, or are they produced through methods such as we know on earth?"

Ashtar: "Both methods are employed. We have on Venus very great alchemists. I am speaking not only for my brothers of Venus, but also for my brothers of other solar systems. I do not speak only of Venus when I speak. There are various methods of producing the provisions which are essential on these rather lengthy journeys of the great ships of space, and they are sometimes placed in condensed form. You see, we do not regard food quite as you regard it. We do not eat food solely for the pleasure, as you do. We know what is essential for the retention of that state of health in our bodies, and we partake the great amount of chemicals and other elements and minerals which are essential to keep our bodies in their perfect shape. Our bodies are of a more etheric nature than yours. They need much less than yours, and so, what would seem enough for two months of earth would take only a fraction of space with us.

"Speaking of foods, I inspired this one to place in readiness what is called a 'pendulum.' She will show you the use of the pendulum to test those foods which have energy for you now and those foods which would best be left aside, which will best retain this higher power, this more subtle energy which we bring when we come. You do understand that, and that therefore it is at least necessary to make gradually certain changes in your habits of food and drink intake.

"You will find it quite interesting, those of you who have not seen the work of the pendulum."

Question: "Does a person have to have any special psychic gift in order to wield the pendulum or could it respond to anyone?"

Ashtar: "Anyone who is in close attunement with their guardian spirit can wield the pendulum. It may take a brief time for attunement, but this one picks it up and asks the question and begins. It is quite simple. You will find it quite accurate and dependable. It is used in many ways, but if you begin with the food testing, the other ways will open to you.

Question: "There is one thing I would like to clear up. I doubt if Ashtar will be willing to do that, for in his talks I have noticed that he refrains from giving any statement which would reflect against any individual, but the question I would like to ask, and it is more for guidance, is this: It is said that sometimes people who claim to be giving information from representatives of the Celestial world do it in the dark, while most of us feel that they should give it in the light."

Ashtar: "There are many means of contact being made by us. The dark is also good. In the darkness of the earth a seed is placed, and out of it, in time, two little tender shoots come forth into the light, so we never criticize and we never condemn. We ask you to weigh it. See if you can find a good in that which is done."

Question: "In one of the books we read recently a Venusian lady was answering questions in which she said that Venusian babies grow up and mature in a period of what we would call two or three years."

Ashtar: "Our evolution and birth cycle is not like yours of

earth. You will learn when you come up here. You will remember more of what is given you when you become more of the texture of that which is given you here. Then it will be retained in the consciousness when you return into your human habitation."

Question: "Do you require sleep?"

Answer: "Oh, yes, we sleep and we rest. We do not permit ourselves to become tense, as you of earth do. We accomplish many things. We, of course, have been blessed by the gift of what you would call 'telepathy,' and what you would call 'projection'; therefore, we can cover greater distances in much less time, but the first secret we had to learn and the first secret you will have to learn is to remain perfectly relaxed."

Question: "There are a number of people who are conscious of a memory of having visited space ships. Is that for any purpose?"

Ashtar: "There is always a purpose in what we do."

Question: "At the close of physical life on your planet when people have fulfilled their mission, I have heard it said they do not die as we do on earth."

Ashtar: "We voluntarily lay aside the mortal form when we know we are ready to take on another evolution. There are evolutions which you of earth are not aware and which it is not wise for us to bring to your consciousness at this time. It would only cause confusion. You have been taken a long way in consciousness—farther than you yourselves realize—but one day it will become clear to you. You of earth will come to that time when you will voluntarily lay down your physical vehicle."

Question: "We have heard so much about the catastrophe on our eastern shores and the question has come up as to whether we should stock our cupboards with food. I understand the Mormons are doing that."

Ashtar: "If you will have the concept in your consciousness that whatever food supplies you have are not for yourself, but for your brother men, then you will be inspired at the right time to know what to do. "

• • •

An unpublished message of encouragement from Ashtar (by Tuella, 1983):

"We come to you in the vibration of Love and Light, sent forth from the upper heavens to penetrate the atmosphere of earth and reach the hearts of all mankind. We enfold the planet with the power of Love and blend into its very layers an annointing of peace and goodwill. We carry away the offcast thoughts of darkness that would destroy your world if left unchecked. We intervene with our own magnetic rays and beams of Greater Light to keep the balance for another decade. White Light is enfolded round and round your world in an essence of purification that will bring the blessings of God upon all nations. Wherever there is a hostile approach to the solution of world problems, our Greater Light will assist to dissolve that hostility and maintain peace. Factions of baser intent are gradually deteriorating and being replaced by understanding and goodwill. Peace will come, and the lesser infiltrations of the dark ones will be overcome. Yield not to weariness of spirit, but continue to watch for our coming and the fulfillment of all the dreams and hopes of humanity for a better world. It will come. Give no place to discouragement in your task. The waters of Life shall flow upon every barren place, and every thirst shall be quenched.

"With victory so very near, do not give up in the battle for the Legions of Light, but carry on in full confidence that the day shall come when war shall be gone forever. From this abyss of seeming hopelessness, a new dawn shall come and a sunrise of Love and a new life shall fill this land. Obtain the promises and hold steady in your battle for the right. Soon these days shall pass, and you shall stand in the beauty of your inheritance. Ashtar has spoken these words."

• • •

Appointments with busy Commander Ashtar are few and far between. They are scheduled at specific times and days near the full moon period. However, at crisis events or on special occasions he does, nevertheless, project to me as he chooses. One of those surprise times came during the routine daily meditation on September 24, 1984.

"Ashtar speaking. I have with me here, at this source of contact, one formerly known to your world as George van Tassel, who will speak to you now."

"Good afternoon, Tuella. I shall refer to myself as George van Tassel, though I am here known by another name. Perhaps in due time this, too, shall be shared with you. I, too, revere and respect the words of that noble first message given to me on his first occasion of addressing our planet directly. That was an honor Ashtar allotted to me, for which I shall always be humbled.

"Since coming, or rather, returning here to 'home base,' it has been a rejuvenating time of blessed constant activity for the good of the Light, especially for the planet earth. I was immediately taken into fellowship with the Great Masters of the Council of which I wrote, and allowed to enter into all of its activities and discussions. This activity still continues. This request by Ashtar to speak with you, his messenger, is a privilege also, which I hasten to fulfill.

"In the coming events upon this planet, there will be a tremendous need of increased communication and contact with the Lords of the higher dimensions. There must now begin upon the planet an attitude of unity and oneness in the great overall communications system between all worlds. There must be in evidence that loving attitude of a desire to share with all, whatever communications are sent, with all others who will receive them. There must be interdimensional exchange such as there has never been before. Those selfish souls who will not enter this exchange for petty and human reasons, will be called upon to answer before the Lords of Karma for their hindering attitudes of lower self in control of their deeds. We can no longer tolerate a resistance movement within the ranks of Light Workers on Earth. Those who resist the coming dawn will become lost on their own wilful pathways. Human differences, human opinions, and human emotional walls must fall before the invading avalanche of God's White Light as it now pours into the vacuum of divisions. New Agers and UFO enthusiasts must blend their energies in an invincible front of force and work together in love for the Great Divine Program of which Ashtar speaks. With the enemy of mankind even at your very doors, this is not the time to be dawdling amongst yourselves and selfishly building your own little kingdoms. The earth faces oblivion while self-centered souls hide their fruits under a bushel bearing their name. There must be inaugurated centers for the dispersion of all information, and a melting pot for dispersement of all major messages from the Space Intelligences. The world is in need of these Extraterrestrial communiques to prepare for the coming transition from the old into the new. Sharing all that you have with one another is decidedly the order of the day for the workers of Light. Let the world look upon your united efforts and see that you are disciples indeed. The world has enough of slanderous attacks, disunity, bigotry and personal pride. It waits to see something better in the World Servers.

"The Confederation, as well as the Federation and the larger Alliance, continuously looks for those units of service which are open in interaction with their fellow brothers and sisters, who envision in terms of the whole, and not certain parts, but rather, flow with one another, aware of their part and portion in an overall program. When these are found, they are immediately blessed and expanded in all of their outreach by the Council and scheduled for greater responsibilities in the time that remains.

"May the love of the Christ within us all flow like a river

throughout all of the land to water the parched ground and prepare for the harvest that awaits. I bid you good day, from one who was George van Tassel."

• • •

In May of 1983 it was my great privilege to have enjoyed one of the finest conferences we have ever undertaken. The vibration of Love was at a high pitch frequency; freedom of the Spirit relaxed and beautifully touched the crowd of over two hundred persons who filled the auditorium. The following blessing was sent to all of them. A young man approached me just before the afternoon session and asked me to accept a message he had received from Ashtar two hours earlier, with the Commander's request that it be read to the audience. I hastened to agree to this, and the following call was directed to each soul present:

"Beloved sons and daughters of the Most High, we give thanks this day that you have come here to Tyler as was planned beforehand. We give thanks to the Father for making all of this possible. We, the brothers of the Ashtar Command, salute you for your love of duty and commitment to the Cause of Freedom for this planet and the system. I am Ashtar, your brother and lecturer this hour, and I come in the name of the Brotherhood to give you your missions.

"Oh sons and daughters of the Most High, rejoice, for your hour of duty to the perfection of the Cosmos is at hand. Arise to the blessings being granted you this day; arise to the responsibilities of your commitments. Each and everyone of you present here at this lecture has volunteered for the coming assignments which will very shortly manifest into your consciousness. Prepare yourselves by keeping in constant tune with your Godselves at every moment of life. Prepare yourselves to raise your individual energies so that the energies may manifest through. Prepare yourselves by keeping your minds attuned only to the pure perfection of God in all things. These things you should now all consider for your individual energies are all important to those commitments of love to your brothers for which you have volunteered.

"I, Ashtar, Commander of the Galactic Fleets now patrolling your skies, do now release to you, our brothers and sisters of Light, in the name of the Most Glorious Son of Our Father, Jesus the Christ, the blessings and energies of beloved Helios and Vesta at this hour.

"I release to you now in the name of the Master Kuthumi, the wisdom necessary to find the means for accomplishing your duties.

"I release to you all now the energies of the Power of the Father through the messenger Archangel Michael and His Legions of Blue Flaming Angels.

"I do release to you now in the name of Master Hilarion, the energy of the ray of Truth, so that you all may know the Truth of Perfection at all times in these next years.

"I, Ashtar, now release to this group in the name of the Ashtar Command's volunteers of Light from all the systems in God's heavens, the Light, Love, and Life of Perfection to release the triggering mechanisms within each and everyone of your souls so that you individually will come to know very shortly your duties to the Father. I, Commander Ashtar, do, at this appointed hour, now release the above God Energies by the power granted to me by My Lord, Esu, in His Father's name, to each and everyone of you worthy of this now! Be it known, oh sons and daughters of our Father, that you have been blessed this moment with Grace of Our Lord to accomplish what will be requested of you soon.

"In the name of the Space Brotherhood, we thank you all now for your devotion to the cause of Freedom for this Earth and this system. We, your brothers, do now salute you all in the name of this cause of Our Most High Source of Perfection for this system. We overshadow you all from this moment onward and do give you all now the prayer that will call those special energies you will all need for your tasks:

> *I, (name in full), do now, by the Authority of the Ashtar Commission for this Earth command in the name of Esu that the necessary energies be released to me now for the accomplishment of my mission. This I call forth now in the name of the Cause, Glory, Effort and Perfection of the Father right here and now. So be it. It is done in the name of Jesus, Lord of the Earth.*

"Use this call to your space brothers whenever you are in need of help, and our protection will at once overshadow you.

"In the Love/Light of the Lord, I do now send forth to you all, my gratitude for your service to the Almighty.

"Go forth now this day with the Energies of Perfection as your shields of power. I am your brother and servant in the Lord, Ashtar, Commander of the Fleets of Heaven."

● ● ●

The messages for Project: World Evacuation *were exhilarating to all of us. For the record, we repeat again a few excerpts from the volume that unveiled the concept of space craft gatherings, for sessions of briefing and training of earth-based volunteers, here using only the messages from Ashtar:*

"We desire to speak to our people. We desire to speak to the Elect of God who have chosen and been chosen to come as volunteers from out of our midst to walk the Earth, to endure the darkness and the challenges and the problems, yea, the temptations; yet to stand and be ready when our call comes to them. As Commander, it is my desire to speak to all of these throughout this hemisphere, as messengers, as teachers, as guidance counselors, as channels of Light and beams of the Love of God to the planet. We have need now to lift you into our presence for a brief moment of time for purposes of special training and many other matters which cannot be handled in any other way. These gatherings shall not be simultaneous throughout the globe, but shall take place in seven various sectors, one at a time. We cannot dispense our forces efficiently by having all of you at once. Therefore, we shall undertake this program in units, by areas, as we have organized other programs in the past.

"We are bringing together those of high leadership status whose responsibilities are far-reaching, and of such a nature that special instructions and training must be given if they are to fulfill their portion of the mission. These have long been in accord with us on inner levels and have spent much time in coordinating necessary discussions relating to their missions while out of body in their night visits with our councils. All of these have sat in on our council meetings while their bodies have slept. Each of you who are to be lifted up in this special gathering have all participated in intergalactic and interplanetary council meetings and listened to preparedness programs. This meeting, in our presence, will take place upon a conscious level. You will retain your full consciousness at every moment and at all times. On this visit you will take with you when you return to Earth situations, a full recall of all that has transpired, along with many evidences of where you have been. Each one of you will be able to prove your sojourn with us, for each will receive undeniable proof to combine with the testimony of many others throughout the globe, presenting accounts consistent with your own. You will be given two objects—one to wear, and one to hold—that will anchor you to that moment for the rest of this embodiment.

"You will return to your earthly situations with a quiet spiritual authority that will never be taken from you and will never forsake you. You will be anointed with spiritual credentials and spiritual abilities representing your badge of initiation and mission. At first, your words will be scoffed at and your reports will bring laughter to the multitudes. But all over the world you will stand together, united in your story, consistent in your report, agreeing in your details, and you will cause them to remove the smiles from their countenances when your credentials are activated. You are the representatives of the Highest Celestial Government and the Highest Council of this solar system, as well as the Highest Tribunal of the Interplanetary Councils. All of us will reinforce each and everyone of you, and you will be convinced of this before you leave our midst to return.

"There are so many of you presently to be lifted, trained and prepared. It is a project of such magnitude that words can scarcely describe not only the effort thus far invested into it over many centuries, but also, the great labor and the millions of volunteers that make it possible.

"Therefore, my closing words to my beloved brothers and sisters of Light in this message is a salute to you in the sign of the Solar Cross. I hold forth my right hand of blessing upon each of you. You know who you are. You know where you stand in your places and your inner guidance. Unfortunately, our words and messages will confuse many, but those who must hear will hear; and those who must see will see. To him that hath ears to hear, let him hear; to him that hath eyes to see, let him see. So be ready, my brethren. Be alert. Be listening, for your call shall come. I am Ashtar, one who commands millions of men in this hemisphere for our Beloved Commander in Chief, Jesus The Christ and the World Saviour."

• • •

Further, in the Evacuation volume, Commander Ashtar discussed details of the global rescue with a poignant logic:
"There is a method and great organization in a detailed plan already near completion for the purpose of removing souls from this planet, in the event of catastrophic events making a rescue necessary. We watch diligently, the threat of a polar shift for the planet in your generation. Such a development would create a planetary situation through which none

could survive. This would necessitate an evacuation such as I have referred to.

"Another manifestation necessitating global rescue would be the collision of an asteroid within your own magnetic field, or the bypass of another solar system. This would so disrupt and disturb your own grid system and energy field that all of the inhabitants of the planet would face extinction. The negativity of man could magnetize these things to himself. Detailed scientific data accumulated over long periods of monitoring the actions of the bodies within the solar system indicates these events are within the realm of possibility.

"This book is not intended to frighten anyone, but on the contrary, to hold out the hope and confidence of our presence with you for any time of trouble. The dangers to the planet are very real. The resulting tragedy to humanity would be unavoidable. However, our presence surrounding you 35 million strong will assist you, lift you up and rescue you, and hold you in safety.

"The magnetized solar flares now present around the sun in its position, in conjunction with the planetary alignment that is presently coming into its final position, combines to create a strong tendency to pull the Earth into untoward motion. The possible polar shift has been greatly lessened and gentled by the action of our scientific volunteers from many worlds. These are greatly learned men who understand these things, and whose services have gladly been given for the purpose of saving this beautiful planet. There are also tracking units with the Ashtar Command which continually trace the pathways of all asteroid action within this solar system and beyond. Any threatening approach of another heavenly body can be strongly averted from its direction. This type of surveillance is constant.

"Inner disturbances taking place within the planet itself are direct reflections of the aspirations and the attitudes and vibrations of those who dwell upon it. We have repeatedly attempted to turn the thoughts of humanity toward the reality of Divine Truth and Principles."

• • •

An evacuation update (through Tuella, June 1984). Commander Ashtar speaks to the date seekers:

"Listen, Eagles: I am here to discuss the question that comes so often to the Light Workers. So many souls still involve themselves in the dates and such, pertinent to their lifting. Although it was explained in our book that no dates could be given, I repeat again that which so many have clearly explained who serve with me, that dates will not be given.

"We are not fortune tellers. We see processes set into motion, energies gathering and gaining momentum; we observe changes weaving their pattern in a situation. However, no member of our Commands nor of the Spiritual Hierarchy can give mankind a certain date, and should such be done, then use much caution and discernment concerning it, for this is not in harmony with things as they are.

"The will of man collectively, events upon the planet, and the possible progression and advancement of the Light as well as the darkness—are all involved in the details of events that would lead to the lifting up and the gathering of the Eagles, as well as the full phases of an evacuation of the planet of the remnant. The importance that must be stressed is not the moment in time, but the preparation for that moment, on the soul level. This is where the emphasis must be placed and is where it will continue to be placed. For one who is totally ready and qualified, there is no need for dates to be given until the very moment has come. Howbeit, in *no instance* will individuals be given long periods of notice for readiness, but only short notices will be given, for security purposes.

"I would ask that this be passed along to the Light Workers; not to seek for a setting of time, but for a thankfulness of an extension of time in which to spread more Light throughout the planet thus to prepare many others. This is the call and the mission, to 'occupy' until He comes Who must come!"

• • •

Finally, we close this brief sampling of messages to Light Workers with this practical message which came through Mrs. E.P. Hill, printed in In Days to Come, *by Saucerian Press:*

"We have been asked to explain the type of cooperation we ask of you. The following suggestions may furnish a clue to our needs. Others will occur to you as you ponder upon the situation in your locality.

"Acquire as much information as possible from all reliable sources, refusing to give credence to any doubts cast upon our sincerity and our ability to carry out orders we receive from our Commander-in-Chief. Without being obtrusively insistent, pass on such information through every channel open to you. It is imperative that the public be alerted to our presence and its purpose. We might remark that treating it as 'news' rather than placing it in a religious category would avoid disapproval in some quarters.

"Use the telephone, private correspondence and casual conversations with friends, or even strangers, to promote a wholesome interest in the subject...tactfully leaving the impression that to deny our existence or doubt our friendly purpose is out of date.

"Encourage the forming of space clubs or small groups to meet at stated intervals for discussion of the latest news available.

"Stress the fact that our first urgent objective must be the removal of the causes necessitating illegitimate use of newly apprehended forces capable of completely disintegrating this planet and doing irreparable damage to *all forms* of living substance in close proximity thereto. We know the extremity reached in the downward course of power-crazed potentates! Under no other circumstances would we have been entreated to undertake our present mission or empowered to intervene and prevent the extermination of the inhabitants of Shan.

"As the opportunity occurs, let your friends know we do not come as adventurers seeking excitement, nor as scientists in quest of fresh knowledge! What could we learn in your laboratories with their passe equipment, or what satisfaction find in the hurly-burly of senseless clashes in mental or physical arenas of action?

"Perhaps it would be well to again emphasize the fact that your inmost thoughts and desires, as well as your acts, create either a very real barrier, or point of contact, according as you reject our way of life (based on the true Christ Principles) or harmonize with our concept of constructive and progressive living. We have passed through a long and tedious process of reappraisal and reevaluation of all Life has to offer in the final analysis, since first we were favored with wise and patient Teachers from 'Outer Space.'

"What they did for us ages ago, we now offer to do for you! It is against every tenet in our code of honor to attempt to force you to accept our services in the capacity of Teachers. Yet this I can promise in all sincerity. Should our offer of genuine, practical assistance be welcome and the necessary preliminary steps be taken, we can and will joyfully pass on to you the knowledge we possess. Not only will we do this, but we will 'loan' you many of our most expert and experienced teachers in every branch of art and industry to initiate you into the secrets we have tried out and proven one hundred percent effective in confidently anticipating a joyous time of rebuilding, remodeling, recreating all things on this earth in perfect harmony and accord with the design and infinitely wise specifications of the Master Architect of the Universe!

"To this glorious and sublime end we pledge our hearts, our minds and every power and skill we possess, till our sacred mission is completed!

"We thank God our mutual success is assured and we

shall see our Beloved Master, the Christ of God crowned King of Kings!

"Unto Him be honor, praise and glory now and forevermore! Ashtar and His Associates from Venus and neighboring planets in loving cooperation with friends on the planet Shan."

Messages to Whosoever Will

Our beloved friend, Ashtar, Commander of the Guardian fleets present in our hemisphere, has expressed some justifiable concern for those to whom spiritual messages from other dimensions and the concept of cosmic telepathy in general, could create negative responses. We who are so familiar with all of these truths tend to forget what it is like to be suddenly exposed to them when one is still in the throes of spiritual underdevelopment. Ashtar speaks to whosoever will listen:

"Perhaps, dear reader, it has never entered your conscious thinking process that one in your dimension can actually communicate with one in higher dimensions through the process of mind to mind thought placement, or 'telepathy,' as it is known. Have you ever seriously considered the possibility of this phenomenon? Can you open your mind to its possibility? Well, then, can we reason together that if it is possible, then it is feasible that some have therefore done so? If some have therefore done so, then it is probable that these messages have been given and received as has been forthrightly stated.

"May we therefore reason further, that if these messages have so been given and received, then man IS capable of higher things than that to which he has hitherto applied his mental abilities. It is an accepted principle that mankind uses but one-fifth of his mental capacities. Why is this so? Is he not further capable of total mental capacity? If not, why not? Earth has programmed its young far too long in an inadequate way, withholding teachings from the toddler until be is a young child, when his mental capacity is ever the same. Precious years of learning are wasted by withholding that learning, when the very young infant is capable of great reasoning power, if you but understood this truism. The inability of the infant to speak audibly is no indication of his mental capacity. In fact, none of you truly need words at all if you would develop the mind to a fuller capacity.

"We have taught those who thus 'hear' us, through long and tedious training sessions of sitting quietly with us, to become receivers of our transmissions. With some such, an ability has to be developed. With others it was present within at birth. Regardless, it is a fact that humankind is perfectly proficient of pure telepathy on the highest level of clarity and perception.

"Let us then accept the validity of the process and consider the fruit of it. Our mental conversations with our messengers are as real as your conversations with anyone you know or love or meet. The telepathic thread of experiencing soundless words within the mind is as lucid and fluent as your own tongue. Do you not also know your friends and loved ones on the telephone by the inflections, the vibrations and tones of their voice, as well as the flow of frequency within your being when that familiar voice is heard? So, likewise, do those with whom we are linked in this fashion, also have those corresponding reactions of recognition and response to one who speaks with them telepathically, when a vibrational form of recognition of the validity of the identification is given. In most of these instances, this kind of communication comes with ease where old ties exist between the transmitter and the receiver, just as there have doubtless been times when in close association with one greatly beloved, you have known each other's thoughts or the words before they were spoken. All of mankind has known these moments, for the original traits are only idle, not removed.

"So you can agree that our method is a valid one; therefore, can you not accept that we are who we say we are and are capable of speaking with you also, and that our identities are true? Ponder on this and do not reject simply because you do not understand or because of unaccustomedness to the presentation. Consider that with God all things are possible. Your researchers have proven that distance, however great it may be, has no effect upon the communication of mind with mind. The power of thought is said to have no limitations or boundaries. Can you build a wall around the thought of a man? You know that you cannot. Thought is as expansive as the universe itself. Therefore, still the body, quiet the mind, and think on us, and we will respond to those who do in love turn thoughts toward us of the Intergalactic Space Confederation.

"All men are capable of cosmic communication. All of humanity is mentally endowed sufficiently to manifest the aspects of the fully opened mind. The human brain is fully adequate to operate in all of its capacity and in all of its inherent functions of sensory perceptions beyond that of the physical senses. There is no paradox here. There is no mystery involved. We are discussing a natural phenomenon not in any way religious, nor superstitious, nor that which must be hidden in the archives of old philosophies. This natural ability is within the scope of all mankind, and not merely by a gifted few.

"The inability of humanity to exercise these divine talents lies in their own misguided concepts and not in their limitations. All of mind is placed at their disposal, requiring only conscious cooperation of the human consciousness.

"The spiritual essence of soul-mind is the key to realization of the fullest potential within the human lifespan. Mentally speaking, mankind is still crawling on all fours, when they are capable of walking tall in the gait of the conqueror. The awakening of the resonating center of the human brain could deliver the earthean society from self-imposed limitations, if they would but apply themselves to these concepts.

"It is an anachronism that in the days of the earth's beginnings, all of these experiences were a part of daily existence, but time and tides in the evolution of men have washed them away. The call reverberates once again for the restoration of human dignity and the upliftment of man into the reality of his Divine Image and His Divine Birthright.

"Furthermore, much is yet to come to pass upon the planet which will necessitate the use of the fullest cosmic awareness in the turbulence of events that can befall this planet. Those who are attuned to Universal Forces will experience their own deliverance through cosmic assistance from the flow of interdimensional communication.

"We pray that the people of Earth will seriously undertake the return to their spiritual inheritance and their true identity in the higher area of consciousness and diligently apply themselves to throwing off the slothfulness of the materialistic thought forms. Arise from the sleep of death and reach for the Life that flows unhindered throughout the universe. This is the call that now comes, and may the Eartheans answer quickly and willingly and set in motion this quest for full spiritual participation in the cosmic language of the universe."

● ● ●

Somehow the plea of Ashtar in this message touches the heart. It helps us to realize the great obstacles our Space Friends face in even attempting to be of help to us.

"I speak for the Most High Command of the Guardian Forces. Preparations are now underway for a great conclave of the Guardian Action. The masses must somehow be reached with an understanding of our true mission and the purpose of our presence in your skies. All fear must be removed from their hearts through teachings that will help them to understand that we surround your planet only in an attitude of love and helpfulness and a desire to serve mankind. Fear of us makes it impossible for the completion of our mission when the time is come.

147

"There are too many who fear us, too many who would withdraw and hold back should an invitation be given to come with us for rescue. We recognize the problem. We are dealing with it in every possible way through hundreds of precious willing souls earth-based. We cannot be of help to those who fear us, who do not trust us, and who cannot accept us. The attitude of humanity must be changed for the great majority, before the hour of crisis. We cannot fulfill the *PLAN OF THE HIERARCHY OR ASSIST MANKIND* unless the world is enlightened to our purpose and mission."

● ● ●

I, personally, have been very impressed with the pointed message on Cosmic Telepathy given by Ashtar as the introduction for their book on that subject published a year ago. It is worthy of isolation here for reconsideration by whosoever will study it:

"The force of telepathic thought is a magnetic force which pulls into itself and sends forth from itself the universal atomic structure of creation. The Mind is the Builder, the thoughts are the building material. Thoughts are catapulted into words, ideas or pictures at your level of reception. Limited though they may be, words are tools of convenience used to describe the energies set into motion by a thought transmitted to the receiver.

"The art of cosmic telepathy is as old as creation itself. Older, only in sequence, are the symbols of reality that preceded it. From the original symbols of communication, thought went forth to forge its own pathway in the worlds of God's creation.

"As humanity returns to the fullness of the stature of MAN, God's creation will master once again the Universal Language of thought transference, through the action of mind.

"The greatest need of the Bearers of Light and those who work with humanity in the coming crisis will be proficiency in the quality of cosmic communications. That hour could come upon the planet when communications will be the lifeline of survival or rescue.

"Blazing a trail for better understanding by using simple diagrams and elementary terminology, we hope to resolve the debris of mystery and ignorance from what should be accepted as normal expression for children of the Creator.

"The general consensus of opinion by those who can only be called ignorant is that a human being is delegated to the physical world and that all that is visible or physically attainable is the only goal of having lived upon this planet. Nevertheless, Light has been consistently and increasingly released into the vortex of Earth for the express purpose of piercing such dark mentalities with an understanding of spiritual concepts that lift human life to its highest plane.

"By the help of the Invisible World of an entire solar system of Spiritual Leaders who administer the Divine Government of your planet from the Great Tribunals, the Earth is constantly bombarded with rays and influences that bring understanding to man's sense of personal worth, an awareness of his potential for greatness, and his ultimate spiritual goal in having entered the dimension at all.

"Included in this tremendous input of possible spiritual attainment is the inherent ability to communicate with his Creator and those of other dimensions who serve His Light. This very natural phenomenon is being brought to the attention of the public at this point in time, to quicken the hearts of those who are destined to find this fulfillment.

"Cosmic Telepathy is the inheritance of the Child of Light. It is the resonating force of illumined Mind, piercing the etheric faster than the speed of Light. It is that power delineated to Man, on Earth or wherever he might be. Universal fellowship is a reality without limitation. Limitation is only made *possible by belief in its existence.*

"We call for the awakening of the sleeping genius within

149

Man to awaken and recognize the Father's image within him. Herein lies deliverance from all limitation and thus, the full potential of Mind will be released to God's Will. Mind's physical counterpart already exists in the unknown 85% portion of his brain. The world is waiting for the men and women who are ready to become all that they are capable of being, in the midst of ignorance run rampant. Awake, thou that sleepest, and the Lord Himself shall give thee Light!

"Gather yourselves together to consider these classic concepts. Your human effort thus invested will be rewarded by the presence and the response of the Hosts of Heaven."

—**Ashtar**

• • •

With highest respect to a great messenger of Ashtar, and his fine work for the Confederation, we share this message received by George van Tassel from Ashtar in August 1952:

"I am Ashtar, in the process of attempting to straighten out numerous conditions that affect this planet Shan. We are going to give you certain information, in the future, that will weld together the two great sciences of your people. I refer to all branches of material science and religion. These two are one in truth, separated only by a gap that we shall give you the key to close.

"In the quadra sector Blaau, man on the planet Shan will have no further use for the misconception that he is faced with in the form of religion, for science of truth, seen and unseen, is the basis of religion, not ancient scriptures, misinterpreted, mistranslated and misconstrued by those who deliver lectures, but based on the true science of life in all phases. Organized scientists are beginning now to explore these realms of the unseen. My love, I am Ashtar."

• • •

During the election campaign of 1984, through the pages

of the Universal Network *newsletter, the people of America received some pertinent and timeless advice from Commander Ashtar on "Choosing a President":*

"Once again America faces its presidential campaign, its opportunity to choose who its leader soul will be in international affairs. We have explained in a recent issue that there are embodied representatives of both the Light and Dark forces in high places in the land. The discernment of the people is crucial in these elective matters. Certain ones are chosen and placed where they are by higher forces. It is incorrect to state that the choice matters not, because of the power of the world manipulators. Light is never helpless against the darkness! One man totally surrendered to the coming of Light and freedom upon this planet, guided and inspired by the contacts of heaven, will be overshadowed, guarded, and counseled every step of his challenging mission. Whatever the challenge, whatever the ultimatum from whatever source, that man who stands in the Light with God is invincible, and in the majority.

"There are times when the American people have not deserved the man who was given them. Other times, through earned karma, they have deserved the leader that was given them. But this November of 1984 is an extraordinary time in the affairs of this nation. Great danger to the American way lurks behind every newscast, every world council, with indescribable repercussions. In the election before you the greatest care and discernment must be applied in choosing the leader who will speak for you in the summit gatherings of the world powers. America must continue to hold her banner high in the face of disregard for human life at all levels, yet maintaining the integrity of honor and respect while standing steadfast in dignity for the rights of free men everywhere. Malignant influences infiltrate the minds of many leaders upon the world scene. America must not compromise her ideals and principles from a basis of fear. Such a platform can degrade the stance of an American leader in the eyes of this and all worlds. When an armor of Light surrounds a great man, it is evident to all in his every word, his deeds and decisions. All responsible leaders of a people should live in the shadow of the Most High, ready in a moment's notice to respond to divine quickenings within his heart. The Spiritual Government of this Solar System is involved in the world politics at this point in time. Decisions that are finalized on your level can affect the entire solar system for good or ill. Therefore, think not that the one who bears the standard for the United States of America this coming November will be entirely your choice and your placement. Higher Intelligences of the Celestial Government will also have their voice in this election. It has been written, 'The powers that be are ordained of God.' Go within thy inner Being and seek the important guidance before you cast your lot for any certain one. Pray unceasingly concerning this coming election. Seek through thy Christed Self to make the choice thy guidance would have you make, placing all of the hopefuls before you in an attitude of prayer. Do not take this particular time lightly, for the world totters on the brink of the results of the decisions of stupid men. The Father knoweth each one of your choices. All may even be good men. But one is best for the world at this time—one with the spiritual stamina and inner dedication to Light which will guide America through its most challenging hour. The fate of the planet, as well as the solar system, could hang in the balance, affected by our choice of that man. We of the Intergalactic Council, who plainly see the hearts, the records of all, plead for your awakened response to the need for God's man of the hour. Listen not to the words of men, the critique of men, bandied forth so blatantly, so unkindly, so unlovingly against their brothers. Turn away thy ear from such chicanery. Be thy own man and think your own thoughts, make your own decisions based upon spiritual *reflection,* the Christ Presence guiding you and your good common sense. Be not like the reed in the wind, but stand upon your understanding of right government for mankind. Be your own thinker, responsible to thyself alone and not to any cartel of pressurized propaganda. Dare to think in consistency with your personal ideals, your private enlightenment and your *mission* to this planet. Dare to invite the forces of heaven to cast their vote *through you* for the soul who must steer this nation through the treacherous shoals just ahead. Be not careless in your response.

"WE, THE GUARDIANS OF TERRA, CALL UPON EVERY LIGHT WORKER WITHIN THE UNITED STATES OF AMERICA TO CONSCIENTIOUSLY SEEK GUIDANCE WITHIN THY INNER CITADEL, NOT MINDFUL OF PARTY NOR POLITICS NOR DISGUISED WORDS. BUT ASK THE FATHER, 'HOW WOULD *YOU* HAVE ME CAST MY LOT IN THIS ELECTION?' EMPTY YOUR MIND, YOUR PROGRAMMED SUBCONSCIOUS, AND LET ONE MAN BE PLACED UPON YOUR HEART. THEN GO FORTH TO YOUR PRIVILEGE, CONFIDENT THAT YOU ARE SERVING THE FORCES OF LIGHT, OVERCOMING HUMAN SELF CHOICES. If all will do this, heaven will be heard in the leadership of this nation. It is time for this great nation to lay aside its castigation of one another, its deplorable charactor assassination in pre-election times, of good men, and its self-willed desires that this is indeed ONE NATION... UNDER GOD! I am Ashtar, leader of the Ashtar Command, of this hemisphere."

Messages of Global Significance

Ashtar Speaks to Men of Earth
(Channeled by Gabriel Green)

"Greetings, people of Earth. I am Ashtar, of the Ashtar Universal Command of Free Planets. I come to you today to give you a brief summary of the total amount of information and guidance that we have given through this channel, Gabriel Green, over the last 13 years.

"To begin with, your planet, the planet Earth, is at a crossroads. Since your people have been given free will—the freedom to express evil as well as good, the choice as to whether your planet and its peoples will transcend this critical period in its evolution and evolve into the New Age relatively non-destructively is a choice that your people must make collectively.

"There is still time, people of Earth, to make this choice and to resolve the many problems that you have been facing for eons of time. But you must act. Freedom is a privilege, and it must be earned. It has been an expression of your people that your people deserve the leaders that they get.

"It has been our purpose to help you as a people, to so see the issues facing your world, that you will select those leaders who can lead you into a more positive direction. We will do our part in helping to inspire and guide and raise the consciousness of your people, so that they can qualify for, and will

154

work to elect, leaders who will have the good of the people at heart.

"You (the Light Workers), over the last three-and-a-half decades, have built an area of understanding and consciousness in millions of people that was not formerly there. So that now there is tremendous potential in the quantity of your people who now have the higher awareness oriented to the needs of *all* the people of your world, rather than to the special interest factions who are served by your present world leadership.

"This *IS* the Time of the End. At the present time you are going through the Last Days of the old Piscean Age. It remains to be seen whether these days become the end of the world for the majority of your people, or the beginning of a glorious New Age that can be manifested within the next few years. If you will follow the guidance that has been given to Gabriel, and to other leaders of your Flying Saucer-New Age Movement, we will be able to help you to transcend this critical period in your evolution, and to enter the New Age in a less destructive fashion.

"There are two main points that you should be aware of:

"1. God's Kingdom is going to be manifested on this earth very soon, one way or another. It will be the free will choice of your people to decide which way will be chosen. One will end your civilization as you presently know it. The other, less destructive way, will help you to evolve through educational processes into the glorious future that will lead you to travel with your brothers and sisters of the stars.

"It is now possible for each of you to contribute to manifesting this Kingdom, if you will put your shoulder to the wheel, and will help to bring God's government into manifestation as it has been given to our ambassador and messenger, Gabriel Green. The Keys to the Kingdom have been given to Gabriel for the purpose of sharing with you details of the way you can participate in helping this Kingdom to now manifest on your planet. The Universal Economic system and the United

155

World (Christ-oriented world government) are 'The Keys to the Kingdom.'

"2. The second important factor, soon to manifest, is the Second Coming of your Christ to the planet Earth. This happening will take place when enough of your people have been raised in consciousness to prepare them for this glorious event. When the gospel (good news) of God's Kingdom on Earth has been preached throughout the world, then the end shall come, or the Second Coming of the Christ of the Aquarian Age shall take place.

"This shall be a wondrous event, shared in by the Angelic Host (millions of your Space Brothers and Sisters from throughout the Cosmos) in their magnificent ships which will be seen in your skies.

"The Christ of the Aquarian Age will arrive in the first public spaceship landing, to be seen by all of your people on international satellite television, and by other advanced scientific processes where such television is not available.

"This shall bring about a wondrous age of change in the lives of all of your people, which has been long awaited and prophesied in your various holy works. There is yet time, people of Earth, for you to bring about the more idealistic and positive transformation of your planet. But you must work together. This is imperative now. You must share in your effort to bring about a non-destructive transformation of all things on your planet—social, economic and political.

"Within the next few years you will be making your choices. So do not hesitate to serve the cause of the Father and His Will for your people. I, Ashtar, of the Free Federation of Planets, Commander of the Universal Confederation of Planets Space Corps, have spoken to you, and give you my love."

• • •

Ashtar's opening words for the Evacuation *manuscript:* *"The Siren Sounds for Mankind."*

156

"In time of war upon the earth, a shrill siren is used to alert the populace that danger is approaching and that they should retire themselves to a place of shelter immediately. We of the Interplanetary Alliance and Space Commands of this hemisphere, known collectively as the Ashtar Command, do now, with the sending forth of this book, sound the siren of warning to mankind.

"Danger is upon you. Drop everything and prepare yourselves. It is time to run toward the shelter of Divine Love and Guidance and to take with you only that which you can carry within the inner citadel of being. The early times of this decade will see the fulfillment of all the prophecies that have been released to the world.

"Down through many cultures, and century after century, we have permitted our Highest and Brightest of souls to come to you and walk amongst you, to teach, to lift and become your friends. You have been taught many things, shown many things, awakened step by step to a higher way of life, an elevated approach to life, and a better way of existence. Precept upon precept, we have lifted you from one level to another.

"Many have benefited and have arisen from their darkness and followed that Light. These have intuitively known that the summons was a call to know themselves and thereby, to undertake that refining of themselves that would reveal the inner divinity. Others have turned their interest elsewhere, ignored the outstretched hand of God, and lifetime after lifetime of opportunity has been squandered by detrimental choices.

"Now it is time to separate these groups in keeping with their choices, and let those who refuse the advancement of their being remain together according to their own desires. The few who have burned within their hearts to find the Ultimate Reality will be permitted to follow these aspirations in the setting of a New World, cleansed and made bright by Universal action.

"Increasingly, we have noticed the tendency of the planet

and its people to pull toward an influence designed to destroy the function of free thinking and freedom of man in making his own choices, governing himself, and managing his national affairs. This diabolical influence has penetrated wholly within every phase of human life and every avenue of world diplomacy and world statesmanship. Predictably, day by day, the freedom of humanity has been infiltrated with that kind of propaganda which ultimately leads mankind away from their pure heritage as sons of God.

"The resulting effects are seen not only in the lives of men, but within the asteroid belt and the planet itself. When humanity stands free, in the full Light of God's Universal Law, all government will be 'of the people and for the people and by the people.' But when the heritage of freedom is destroyed, mankind becomes as puppets on strings, stripped of honor, life, strength, forthrightness and glory!

"The Heavenly Father has placed within the burning center of man that likeness of Himself which enables man to govern himself in righteousness and peace. The destruction of this center has been the goal of the Destroyer. Now the forces of Light and Righteousness must rise to the defense of humanity before it is too late. This is the primary action taking place behind the visible scene surrounding all of life.

"Now, all levels of life will be highly raised in frequency, and all manifestations of lower life will wither and dissolve and be removed from the visible scene, to reconstruct the Father's Plan for this beautiful planet. A new fresh start for man is in the making! The astral belts will be purged, the heavens will be cleared, the nature kingdom will find its true destiny and humanity will be glorified in keeping with the Father's design. This is coming to pass in your generation. There is no time left to dally and consider. The hour of decision for a planet is not only come, it is almost gone.

"So it is, the 'siren sounds' for mankind, and there is silence in heaven for that moment that now is, when this great separation shall take place. You who read are versed in the spiritual verities involved. This book will clarify human consciousness concerning the future on your octave. Read...and understand."

—**Ashtar**

• • •

Trevor James tells us:
"The following communication came immediately following the much publicized and much delayed airdrop blast at Eniwetok, in the 1956 series of tests:"

Ashtar: "Scientists at Eniwetok have exploded yet another fission device. You have already experienced the drop in temperature. There will be more. There will be considerable climactic havoc on your surface. The effect of fission upon the weather is obvious to everyone except the scientists, who do not *wish* to believe what is obvious to the simplest entity. Your scientists are not satisfied with the sun they have been given, but prefer to make their own. The Creator's work is not good enough for them. This prospect fills us with sorrow.

"The tone of this communication is one of resignation, as though the personality concerned could hardly bear the contemplation of what was happening. With it all, there was the strange atmosphere of inevitability."

He has also told this messenger:
"Cleansing is unavoidable. Change is inevitable. Wherever there is progress, there has been change. In the New Age of enlightenment, purity shall prevail."

• • •

Gray Barker, of the Saucerian Press, summarizes the messages of Ashtar:
"They all, without exception, warn of impending disaster if mankind does not adopt a more tolerant and understanding attitude among nations and peoples, and cease the hydrogen bomb and armament race."